Can YOU LOVE YOUR-SELF?

Self-Esteem for Today's Woman

JO BERRY

A Division of GL Publications
Ventura, California, U.S.A.

To Georgia Lee and Jo
for the example they were to me.

Other good Regal reading:
Don't Look Now But Your Personality Is Showing by Ethel Barrett
How to Cope by Lloyd H. Ahlem
Your Churning Place by Robert L. Wise

The translation of all Regal books is under the direction of GLINT. GLINT provides technical help for the adaptation, translation and publishing of books for millions of people worldwide. For information regarding translation contact: GLINT, P.O. Box 6688, Ventura, California 93006.

© Copyright 1978 by GL Publications
All rights reserved

Sixth Printing, 1983

Published by Regal Books
A Division of GL Publications
Ventura, California 93006
Printed in U.S.A.

Library of Congress Catalog Card No. 77-089395
ISBN 0-8307-0579-1

CONTENTS

INTRODUCTION

One of the saddest quotations in all of literature is Thoreau's, "The mass of men lead lives of quiet desperation." How true that is. So many people are devoid of the precious motivating commodity called self-esteem. This book is written to help you assess and develop your worth as a human being.

I am convinced that the God who "so greatly loved and dearly prized the world that He [even] gave up His only-begotten [unique] Son" (John 3:16, *AMP*) to save us doesn't want anyone, especially His children, going through life downtrodden, depressed or impotent, thinking of themselves as unworthy worms.

This was a difficult study to prepare. First I turned to my own life to see how, despite some morbid circumstances, I'd gotten my sturdy self-image. I talked to

5

other men and women who appeared to have a proper approach to their value as individuals. None of us could pinpoint a specific formula. There was no three-point outline. We came from varied socio-economic backgrounds and home situations, but there was one common factor: each of us had been exposed to someone(s) who valued us enough to create a sense of self-worth within us; so we possessed a deep-seated determination not to give up on ourselves, even if everyone else did.

My next step was to search Scripture for ideas and theories about self-image. I knew I couldn't go to a concordance or topical Bible, open it up and look under "S." So I had to really study Scripture, always searching for clues to self-image. I found the same common factor I'd already discovered: those who appropriated God's power, discovered that He valued them enough to create in them a sense of self-worth; He imparted in them a deep-seated determination to never give up on themselves because He never would.

This study offers no easy answers or simple solutions to what may be lifelong problems, but it does contain suggestions that, when you apply them, can make you think and feel better about yourself. In it we stress the importance of making positive changes. We take into account the immense impact that being liked and accepted by others can have on your self-esteem.

This is a self-help book. You can study and work through it by yourself or in a study group. But don't think you can settle back with a cup of tea, put your feet up, relax and browse through it. You have to do something all the way through. So keep a pencil handy.

Although I've drawn on personal analogies from my life and the experience of others, the ideas and principles set forth herein are based on Scripture. They are what God's Word teaches us about self-image. Therefore they work. They are true. They are adequate. They are usable. My prayer is that they will help you.

Jo Berry

THE POSSESSIVE PAST

Once upon a time there was a little girl. Her mother and daddy were kind, understanding parents who loved her so much. They taught her that she had been born for a very special purpose. They didn't tell her what that purpose was but they began to prepare her. They taught her to set goals and achieve them. They told her she was sweet and pretty and of great value. They gave her the gift of herself as a person.

Then one day, when she was 13, suddenly and tragically, her parents were killed. She was left alone—well not really alone. Two people said they wanted to help her. They became her guardians. But they didn't know she was born for a special purpose and were only interested in the money from her parents' estate. They made the little girl think she was put on earth only to make their lives miserable, that she was of no value to anyone and whatever good she did was not of much consequence.

The girl tried to make them love her but they weren't interested in her love. They told lies about her to the rest of her family and friends saying that she did bad things and acted immorally. They told her she was ugly and selfish, and they were very cruel to her. It seemed they deliberately set about to destroy her dignity and crush her spirit.

Now the girl was really alone. One night she cried out into the darkness, "I'll just go ahead and be what they say I am. It doesn't matter. No one cares anyway."

But in the quiet darkness her heart echoed back, "That's not true. You care."

She heard her mother's and father's voices: "You have been born for a special purpose." "You're a sweet girl." "We're so proud of you, honey."

Right then, she purposed in her heart to be true to the legacy of love her parents had given her: the gift of herself as a person. No amount of pain, indignity nor condemnation could erase those first 13 years.

So she re-gathered the chipped pieces of her dignity, glued them together with what little courage she had, salved her wounded spirit with righteous indignation and then proceeded to live her life as fully and capably as she could.

I was that girl. Why didn't I fall apart as others have in such circumstances? Why didn't I contemplate suicide or run away from home? Why did I stick it out against overwhelming odds? Reflecting back, I really believed I could overcome any situation. I wouldn't let anything overcome me. I had dreams, I had goals to reach and, although I was only 13 years old, I wasn't about to let "them," whoever they were, destroy my life. I was determined to survive.

I've known other people who made it also. Susie is a vivacious extrovert who has many friends and is an exciting person to be with. She's composed, kind and considerate. If I had to pick one word to describe her it would be *confident*.

Susie's mother died when she was four years old. Her father was an alcoholic. She was shipped from cousin to cousin until she graduated from high school when she was expected to get out on her own. She went to business school, became an executive secretary, and is now in college working on a degree in psychology. Susie came from a deprived background yet she had tremendous self-image.

I've also known people who didn't have difficult circumstances to battle; but they didn't make it. Dan is a shy, non-exertive man. He shuts himself away from interpersonal relationships. He has acquaintances but no close friends. He's just part of the crowd. He has held the same position in the same company for 12 years. Others with less experience and seniority pass him by on the ladder to success. He's a good worker but never seems to get anywhere. If I had to pick one word to describe Dan it would be *unsure*.

Dan comes from a well-to-do, socially prominent family. His parents are warm, loving people who doted on their only son. He's had all the advantages of a nice home and good schools. He dropped out of college after his second year and settled into what appears to be a lifetime rut. Dan comes from what most of us would

11

consider an ideal environment but he has a poor, insufficient self-image.

Self-Image: What Is It?

Many of us equate the word self with selfish. Actually, self is simply another word for me—a name I call myself. An image is a reflection; something we see mirrored to us in one form or another. So self-image is a reflection of me to myself.

When you stand in front of a mirror you look at yourself and the mirror reflects a physical image back to you. When you stand before your mental mirror you view yourself and your mind reflects a mental portrait back to you. That is your self-image.

Write your definition of self-image.

How do we get our self-image? Where does it come from? As I read books on the subject and talk with people about their self-image, I find that everyone has a different answer. I'll tell you where I believe self-image comes from. Few of us can remember the first three or four formative years of our lives and I'm convinced it is in those tender, newest moments that a child receives a basic concept of self-esteem.

The way mother approaches her child, touches him, speaks to him, can say, "You are valuable," or it can say, "You aren't worth much." The way dad guides his child through intimate contact, the way he shows concern declares to the child, "You are of personal worth to me and to yourself," or "You are in the way; you aren't important."

Before Susie *Confident* was born, her mother wanted a baby very badly. She was delighted when her daughter was born. Even though she had just a few years with Susie she spent quality time with her little girl, not out of duty but out of love.

Dan *Unsure's* parents weren't ready for the responsibility of a child when he was conceived. They gave him a lot of things but, perhaps, somehow in the way they held him, spoke to him and approached him he sensed that unspoken word—rejection. Without meaning to they silently said, "We love you but—"

So in those very early years, your parents, or other people in your life, instill in your heart the way you see yourself. They let you know who you are and what is expected of you as a child.

For example, adults who perform with confidence were usually, as children, expected to achieve. Parents don't always extract these high expectations the same way but the result is the same. One little girl may have been yelled at and spanked whenever she didn't try to reach a goal her father set for her while another was verbally reassured and commended for her efforts and encouraged to try again. But both were expected to achieve. As children they were trained to perform and as adults, they still do. They appear to be the kind of people who see problems, not as insurmountable obstacles, but as opportunities. There was instilled within them the idea that they must set goals and strive to reach them. Try, try, try, try! Even if they don't succeed

13

they do all they can. The image of "capable doer" was computed in them as children and this image contributes to their self-worth.

What Image Do You Have of Yourself?

What kind of a self-image was instilled in your life? List several ideas you have about yourself, such as, "I'm lazy," or "People think I'm fun to be with." Think of both good and bad aspects. When you finish your list read each good or positive one and write a way you can enhance it. For example, if people think you're fun to be with you could enhance that positive by making a special effort to visit shut-ins who are lonely, by accepting a leadership position in a club or by becoming a teacher's aide at the local school. Enlarge your sphere of operation.

Read each bad or negative characteristic and list one way you might start to change it for the better. If laziness is your problem, promise not to procrastinate on one item but do everything that has to be done when it needs to be done. Complete every task you undertake.

Negative me   *Approach to change*

Positive me   *Approach to enhancement*

God created each of you as you are. Psalm 139 says He, as Master Designer, fashioned you from the inside out while you were in your mother's womb. He intricately and caringly wove your chromosomes and genes into the person you are. He "fearfully and wonderfully" made you into the end product received by your parents when you were born.

God is pleased with His creation. Genesis 1:31 says, "And God saw all that He had made, and behold, it was very good." Now it is your responsibility not to pervert or destroy how God created you, but to enhance and build upon His original perfect creation. If He declared His creation good then you must accept the idea that God wants you to believe you are good and develop a good self-image.

His Word gives the formula for developing an appropriate opinion of yourself: "Don't cherish exaggerated ideas of yourself or your importance, but try to have a sane estimate of your capabilities by the light of the faith God has given to you all" (Rom. 12:3, *Phillips*). We find in this verse two ways to approach self-image: a wrong way and a right way. First, you are told what not to do.

"Don't cherish exaggerated ideas of yourself or your importance." In other words, don't be egotistical or superficially proud.

God never tells us *not* to do something without also giving positive direction. So, consistent with His loving character, He presents the other side to us and tells us what we're supposed to do: "Try to have a sane estimate of your capabilities by the light of the faith God has given to you all."

Egotism Is Harmful to Self-Image

What happens when a person is prideful and selfish rather than approaching herself in a sane manner? Oddly enough, her self-image suffers. Proverbs 16:18 aptly states, "Pride goes before destruction, and a haughty spirit before stumbling." If you think too highly of yourself you'll get hurt.

The book of Esther tells the story of a man who made the mistake of doing just that. His name was Haman. When King Ahasuerus appointed him to a high position in the court, Haman expected all men to bow down and worship him. He had such an exaggerated idea of himself he felt he deserved something that God alone should receive.

One religious Jew, Mordecai, refused to bow to any man and Haman was filled with rage and set out to destroy all the Jews, as vengeance against Mordecai. He even constructed a gallows on which to hang his enemy. His evil plot eventually backfired because the king discovered that Mordecai had helped to overthrow a plot against his life and decided to honor him.

So King Ahasuerus called Haman in and asked his opinion of what should be done to honor a worthy sub-

ject. Because Haman cherished an exaggerated importance of himself he assumed the man the king wanted
to honor was Haman himself. Esther 6:6 says, "Haman
said to himself, 'Whom would the king desire to honor
more than me?' "

So Haman suggested, "For the man whom the king
desires to honor, let them bring a royal robe which the
king has worn, and the horse on which the king has
ridden, and . . . a royal crown . . . and let the robe and
the horse be handed over to one of the king's most noble
princes and let them array the man whom the king
desires to honor and lead him on horseback through the
city square, and proclaim before him, 'Thus it shall be
done to the man whom the king desires to honor' "
(Esther 6:7-9).

You can imagine Haman's shock when the king told
him to do all those things for Mordecai.

And even that humiliation wasn't enough. Later the
king found out from Queen Esther, who was a Jewess,
about Haman's plot to kill all the Jews. And the king
ordered Haman hanged on the gallows he'd built for
Mordecai. Esther 7:10 records the end of Haman's
prideful downfall: "So they hanged Haman on the gallows which he had prepared for Mordecai, and the
king's anger subsided."

The moral of that story could appropriately be the
first words of Romans 12:3, "Don't cherish exaggerated
ideas of yourself or your importance" (*Phillips*).

Inferiority Feelings Also Harm Self-Image

At the other end of the spectrum, opposite egotism,
is what psychologists call an inferiority complex or
thinking too little of yourself. False humility and debas-

ing yourself can be just as destructive as being puffed up with pride.

One of God's greatest leaders suffered from a poor self-image. The Lord called Moses to lead His people (see Exod. 3:16-22) and Moses' first reaction was one of fear and uncertainty: "What if they [the people] will not believe me, or listen to what I say? For they may say, 'The Lord has not appeared to you'" (Exod. 4:1).

God showed him how he could handle that problem so Moses came up with another reason why he couldn't do what God asked. "Please, Lord, I have never been eloquent, neither recently nor in time past, nor since Thou hast spoken to Thy servant; for I am slow of speech and slow of tongue" (4:10).

Moses is certainly trying to prove his point—he isn't capable of leading. After all, how can someone who can't verbally communicate lead an entire nation? That's a logical argument, isn't it? Sounds reasonable, just as many of our cop-outs are reasonable and logical. But is it an acceptable excuse?

What is God's response? He says, "Who has made man's mouth? Or who makes him dumb or deaf, or seeing or blind? Is it not I, the Lord? Now then go, and I, even I, will be with your mouth, and teach you what you are to say" (4:11,12).

I don't know about you, but that would have convinced me. However, Moses' inferiority feelings ran so deep, possibly like those you have, that even God's dynamic promise couldn't negate his feelings of inadequacy. So he argued further, asking the Lord to send someone else. Even then, although the Bible says "the anger of the Lord burned against Moses" (4:14), God didn't allow Moses to back out. Instead, He called

18

Moses' brother Aaron to speak for him and still insisted that Moses lead the Israelites, which he did successfully.

There is a great lesson in this story. God wants to use you. He is able to help you fully develop your potential, but you have to believe God can do that work in you. Because of Moses' unbelief he missed the blessing of seeing God overcome his speech handicap. Yet he did achieve and became a dynamic, revered leader.

As was the case with Moses, the only limits you face in overcoming a poor self-image are the ones you impose on yourself. You must turn loose of past ideas and trust Almighty God to give you the ability to make a sane estimate of the capabilities He's created in you.

Are you guilty of using the same kind of "I can't do this because" arguments that Moses used? The world calls them cop-outs; I'll call them "Moses' excuses." Below are some common ones. Read the excuse then rephrase it to say exactly what is implied in the statement. Next, write a sentence giving a brief plan of action you could take to prevent or overcome the predicted outcome.

Here is an example: "I'll be lucky to pull a D in this class. I'm just no good at math."

Implication: "I'm going to get a bad grade in this class no matter what I do."

Plan of Action: Study extra hours; hire a tutor; set a goal to get at least a C.

1. "I couldn't accept a position as an officer in the club. I'd never be able to do the kind of job the outgoing president has done."

Implication: I'm introverted & not as qualified so I won't even try.

19

Plan of Action: put your best foot forward & try your best - be yourself & not try to live up to someone else's expectations

2. "I had a good idea to share with the publicity committee but I didn't. For some reason I seldom get a chance to speak up at the meetings and when I do no one listens."

Implication:

Plan of Action:

3. "I like to teach the class but I think I'd better say no. I could never teach as well as Mary does."

Implication:

Plan of Action:

Do you ever use "Moses' excuses"? Actually, they keep you from seeing yourself as you really are. I remember when I was a little girl, one of the things I loved most was going to the carnival when it came to town. I anticipated riding the Ferris wheel and gorging on delicious pink, fluffy cotton candy. But best of all I

20

liked the house of mirrors. I'd spend hours in it. I'd quickly pass by the mirrors that made me look fat and stumpy and linger before the ones that reflected a tall, willowy girl who could have eaten pounds of fudge and still remained slim.

"Look at me," I'd giggle. But I knew it wasn't me; it was an illusion—something I wished I was. Yet, for that brief moment, I'd play the game and bask in what I appeared to be.

It's difficult to look at yourself as you are. Frequently we, like children in a house of mirrors, quickly pass by the flaws we don't want to face in ourselves and linger before the illusions that portray us as we wish we were. So we play games with life and bask in what we appear to be, never honestly facing ourselves.

As I teach about self-image I frequently ask women to write five words or phrases to describe *who* they are. Consistently, they list what their role is. The answers come back: wife, mother, secretary, golfer, teacher. That's not what people *are*; that's what they *do*.

Why is it so difficult to state who you are; what you are like in temperament, personality and character? Why can so few people describe themselves? I'm convinced it's because they never think about themselves in intimate, personalized terms. Linda summarized it beautifully when she said, "I don't know me: I'm much better acquainted with what I do than who I am."

Will the Real Me Please Stand Up?

To discover the real you, you must first discover how you see yourself. Can you list five adjectives that paint a verbal self-portrait of how you see yourself? Are you happy, inhibited, carefree, unstructured, impatient—?

1.
2.
3.
4.
5.

Your list undoubtedly contains both positives and negatives. The positives are the strengths you'll want to amplify; they're the things that make you feel good about yourself. But what about the negatives, the things with which you're dissatisfied that detract from your feeling of self-worth?

The Scriptures have a suggestion on how to re-program negatives into positives: "Do not live any longer ... blindfold[ed] in a world of illusion ... fling off the dirty clothes of the old way of living ... put on the clean fresh clothes of the new life" (Eph. 4:17-24, *Phillips*). The life-changing principle in this verse is: *It's easier to act yourself into a new way of thinking than to think yourself into a new way of acting.*

Don't let futile thoughts control you. Instead, *act* contrary to the worthless, useless, unfair ideas you've formulated about yourself. If you lose control of your thinking your actions are affected. Conversely, if you *act* properly it affects how you think.

For example, when we become impatient we tend to rush around. Instead, move slowly; walk rather than scurry. Purposely act contrary to your impatient feelings and you'll find you're actually more patient. Your *walk* has revised your thought pattern. Or, if you need to lose 10 pounds, you can think incessantly about dieting; but unless you act differently toward food and stop eating so much you'll never lose weight.

Psychologists call this kind of action *behavior modifi-*

cation but it's been buried in the Bible for centuries. For example, Deuteronomy 5:33 tells us to walk in the way of the Lord so that we will live longer and all may be well with us; Romans 8:4 says to walk after the Spirit, not after the flesh. If you want your life set on life and peace, modify a negative walk for positive results.

So, as you look at yourself, if there are things you see that you don't like, you can change them by acting differently; act contrary to your thoughts about yourself. If you're shy, purposely sit in the front row or instigate a conversation with the most popular person in the room. Don't withdraw or hold back, act gregarious and self-assured.

If you're so forceful you frighten people, rather than spouting your 10 favorite pet theories, listen to someone. Strike up a conversation with a person who looks like a potential wallflower. Conduct yourself in a gentle, unassuming manner.

Sometimes when I suggest this approach people ask, "But isn't that being a hypocrite?" It isn't. You're being a hypocrite if when you are angry you pretend not to be, or if you're impatient you claim you're a person who never gets frazzled. What I am suggesting is that you change the way you react to what you think or feel, not that you act phony or force yourself to be something you aren't. If you're angry, admit the anger but choose to handle it in an acceptable way. If you are impatient, don't disclaim it but don't give in to it.

In his book, *The Christian Use of Emotional Power*, H. Norman Wright explains the principle this way: "While we usually are not able to control an emotional response to a particular stimulus, we *CAN* control how we express that emotion. If you feel hate, you do not have to act hateful.... Even if you do react out of a habit pattern you can choose to react differently and try a new pattern."[1]

As you replace negative traits with positive ones, you will see yourself differently and start changing your self-image.

The second thing you must do to discover the real you is to find out how others see you.

Everyone is susceptible to the opinions of others. We want to be liked and accepted so we are vulnerable, sometimes to the extent that we are hurt or wrongly influenced by friends, acquaintances, neighbors or colleagues. Remember, God's Word says you are to make a *sane estimate* of your strengths and weaknesses.

We are all human, therefore apt to err. You have some valid ideas about yourself and some that are wrong or incomplete. Other people may have distorted opinions about you or may vividly see character flaws and assets of which you are unaware. So you openly but selectively accept what people think about you. Whether someone offers a compliment or criticism, you must objectively evaluate all verbal and nonverbal communication to you about yourself. If you automatically discard those things with which you disagree or only welcome comments and attitudes that confirm your present beliefs you'll never grow or change as a person.

If you retain set ideas and a non-receptive, don't-try-to-change-me attitude, you will stunt your emotional growth. Only an occasional weed can grow through cement, but there is fertile soil in an open mind. Reflect back over the past three months and recall some compliments and criticisms that were given to you. Think about each one. Was the criticism or compliment valid?

24

Fair? Neutral? Did you discard it only after careful consideration or did you toss it away hastily, defensively, because you don't want to face the possibility of having to change?

Do You Have a Distorted Self-Image?

Self-image is seeing yourself as you understand yourself to be. You paint a mental picture of yourself, for yourself, and act according to it. If the picture, or your self-opinion, is *distorted* you have a bad self-image.

Annie is a capable, sharp woman. She's an excellent counselor and has a charm that makes people immediately responsive to her. Yet she sees herself as unpopular and inadequate because she spent her teenage years under the shadow of a shallow but beautiful older sister. So Annie has an untrue, poor self-image and is rendering herself impotent. Perhaps you are doing what Annie did.

Conversely, if the mental thought-picture you paint of yourself is *realistic* you're going to have a good self-image. Note that the picture doesn't have to be pretty or perfect but *realistic*.

We find, in literature, an example of the destructiveness of an unrealistic self-image. Greek mythology tells the story of Narcissus, who was exceedingly beautiful and totally vain. He was incapable of any emotion except self-love. He was devoted to adoring and admiring himself.

Someone else loved him too. A dainty lass named Echo. But he was so consumed with himself that he never noticed her great love for him. She was so saddened that she pined away to a mere voice—an echo.

Nemesis, who observed all this, was so appalled by

Narcissus' egotism that he decided to punish Narcissus for his coldness of heart. He devised a plan. Nemesis lured Narcissus to a certain fountain, which was full of crystal-clear, mirror-like water. When Narcissus saw his reflection he was so enamored with himself that all he could do was stare into the pool. He stared and stared, seized with a passion for himself. He stared so long that he was destroyed as a man and was transformed into a flower—the one, according to the myth, that bears his name—the narcissus.

Echo was unrealistic in her approach to self because she let someone affect her to the extent that she negated herself—she became a "nothing." Narcissus, in startling contrast, was so taken with himself he never discovered who he was or what he was capable of becoming, which was also self-destructive.

Is your self-image realistic? Do you see yourself primarily in a negative way or as almost perfect? Neither is realistic. You have strengths and weaknesses, some negative patterns where improvement is needed and some positive aspects on which to build. If you refuse to acknowledge either the bad or the beautiful in yourself you cannot grow, improve or change.

The greatest detriment to developing a realistic self-image is refusing to see negative areas that need to be changed or positive characteristics that can be beneficial to yourself and others. It isn't easy to face yourself. You cannot do it alone, so you must call upon the One who created you and who can help you formulate a proper self-image.

Perfecting the Good Work

Philippians 1:6 says, "I am confident of this very

thing, that He who began a good work in you will perfect it until the day of Christ Jesus." If you, by an act of your will, put your faith in God, He in turn will begin within you the good work of forming and changing you into all you're capable of becoming, all He created you to be. He will continue transforming you toward the ultimate perfection, the image of Christ, which will be fully accomplished when you meet Him face to face.

Are you ready to take a realistic look at yourself? There are three questions you might ask that will help you see yourself: Who am I? What am I like? Why do I do what I do?

Your response to "who am I?" can be defined as your character. Character is your values, your moral standards and the way you respond to your conscience. The values you possess and act upon, such as honesty, sincerity, integrity, fairness, loyalty, humility, or selfishness, injustice, deviousness, all compose your character. For example, I know my husband would never lie to me. He is, and always has been, the most honest person I have ever known. His character is such that he does not and will not lie or deal falsely.

Your response to "what am I like?" can be defined as your personality. Are you an introvert or an extrovert? Are you competent, efficient and organized or lackadaisical and able to operate with loose ends hanging? Are you sporty or a bookworm? Do you prefer chocolate or vanilla? Crowds or a small intimate group? All reflect your personality; they are traits that make you different from everyone else.

Character and personality are not necessarily compatible. A delightful personality can conceal a lousy character. Likewise, you may be a pillar of virtue yet not

27

classify as a charmer. People can possess similar character assets yet have quite different personalities or be alike in personality but have dissimilar characters.

"Why do I do what I do?" is whatever motivates you. Why do you act and react in certain ways? Your response to that question sums up your performance.

Why did Sally always quit whatever she undertook before she finished it? Why, when she was doing a superb job as membership chairman for the PTA, did she resign without a reason three weeks before the close of the campaign? Why, when she was nearing the finals, did she drop out of the tennis tournament? Why does she have several items of clothing stuck away in a dresser drawer, half sewn, although she is an excellent seamstress and could use the clothes?

Sally analyzed why she did these things. She decided it was because as a child she lived with a maiden aunt who was never pleased or satisfied with the results of Sally's performance, so Sally just quit producing. Backing out was easier than facing criticism and failure. In adulthood, she had an image of herself as a quitter, an undependable person. When she realized what motivated her to stop short of goals she truly wanted to reach, she was able to cast aside her childhood behavior pattern and perform up to her capabilities. Her self-image improved.

Who are you? What are you like? Why do you do what you do? Are you a little child in a house of mirrors, dealing only in illusions? Or are you, like Sally, casting aside childhood behavior patterns that adversely affect your self-worth? Are you willing to start looking at yourself as you *are*, so you can become what you want to be?

The apostle Paul makes a practical observation in 1

Corinthians 13:11. He says, "When I was a child, I used to speak as a child, think as a child, reason as a child; when I became a man, I did away with childish things." As you look at yourself as you are, if you desire to become a woman in the fullest sense, do as Paul did. Stop speaking, thinking and reasoning as a child. Do away with childish opinions and ideas of yourself. Take a realistic, positive, helpful look at what you are really like.

REMEMBER: IT'S EASIER TO ACT YOURSELF INTO A NEW WAY OF THINKING THAN TO THINK YOURSELF INTO A NEW WAY OF ACTING!

Workshop
Let's build on positives! First list five things you do well. Don't discount little things like making the best pie crust in the world, being the best weed puller in your family or being the only gal in your office who makes coffee that everyone loves.

1.
2.
3.
4.
5.

Now, write one sentence stating how each of these contributes to the happiness of yourself and others. For example, being the best coffee-maker in the office means you get some well-earned praise and your co-workers get good coffee to drink!

1.
2.
3.

4.

5.

Refer back to the five adjectives you included in your verbal self-portrait on page 21. Pick a negative one that bothers you about yourself and write it here.

Now, write several things you can do to act yourself out of being that way. For example, if you are impatient you could list, "Count to 10 before I speak or act, walk slowly, remember all the problems my impatience has caused in the past and think of a calm solution."

Notes

1. H. Norman Wright, *The Christian Use of Emotional Power* (Old Tappan, NJ: Fleming H. Revell Co., 1974), p. 17.

THE 2
HEART OF THE
MATTER

Are you becoming more aware of yourself as a person, what your character and personality are like? If so, it's time to start making some changes that will improve your self-image. But where do you begin?

You could start with the most obvious, the outer you —buy a new wardrobe or get your hair restyled. Or, you could change what you do—enroll in Yoga classes at the local college, join a new club or take up golf. None of these will prove satisfactory, however, because the same old you will still lurk beneath the new facade. The place to start forming the new you is internally.

Your opinion of yourself affects all areas of your life. A new acquaintance steps into your living room and says, "I knew you'd decorate in yellows and oranges; they fit your personality." Your home reflects you. The clothes you wear, the colors and styles you choose are unspoken statements about the kind of person you are. So is your job or profession and your choice of a boyfriend or husband.

The factors that determine your feelings of self-worth have been built slowly and methodically into your heart. You didn't develop as a person overnight but are a composite of all the bits and pieces of trivia and trauma you've lived through since your birth.

Think of yourself as a computer. Negative and positive data have been fed into your memory bank from the moment you were born. Many programmers have participated in this feeding-in process. When you were young you had little control over the data you received or the person who input it. As a child, for the most part, you were subject to your environment. You didn't choose your parents, where you lived or your life circumstances.

As you matured, you were able to select or reject certain data and to exert more control over your environment. The number and quality of facts, emotions and reactions you have experienced, which have brought you to this point in time, are mathematically astounding. Nevertheless, you are engulfed and possibly trapped in them.

The Feeding-in Process

What are some deciding factors that are compiled in your heart that have given you the image you have of yourself today?

The first of these is the biological factors. These are your inherited characteristics. They were inputted into you at the time you were conceived, through your genes and chromosomes. They determined your sex, the color of your hair and eyes, body stature and all inherited tendencies such as baldness or diabetes. You couldn't control these factors, but Psalm 139:13 says they were imparted to you by a sovereign God. "THOU didst form my inward parts; THOU didst weave me in my mother's womb. I will give thanks to THEE for I am fearfully and wonderfully made."

Obviously, your creation wasn't dictated by chance. You were formed by God's gracious design, not by genetic accident.

Your autonomic nervous system acts and reacts independently of your conscious thoughts but affects the condition of your heart. When you're walking you don't consciously think, "Now I will put my left foot forward, now my right." Breathing and heartbeat are involuntary actions. Pain is instantaneous. You don't have to mentally judge whether or not you are hurting when you hit your thumb with a hammer or splatter hot grease on your arm. Your biological nervous system can cause you to react automatically in certain ways without your being aware of why you are doing it.

Environmental factors also influence your self-image. You react to outside stimuli so your surroundings influence your opinion of yourself. Do you picture yourself as relaxed or formal? City slicker or country naturalist? A live-and-let-live type or a demanding perfectionist? Are material possessions important to you or do you place little value on them? Such attitudes are the result of your response to your environment.

You will consciously or unconsciously, in both negative and positive ways, partially model yourself after various people who touch your life. Your primary models were your parents. Their influence was permanent and powerful because during your most pliable, formative years they mirrored to you a concept of who you are. They helped form your character values and personality traits.

Have you ever heard someone say, "She's her father's child" or "He's just like his mother?" You are a composite profile of those closest to you. Teachers, friends and even celebrities you admire also help program your behavior as you follow patterns you pick up from them.

Although these physiological and psychological factors presently affect who you are, they can be changed or removed. They are not permanent demons. Some experts would have you believe that once you are basically formed as a person there is nothing you can do to change things. They lament that you are totally at the mercy of your environment, controlled by the impersonal whims of a decadent, selfish society and that you have everyone but yourself to blame for your problems and lack of self-esteem.

Is that true? Are you totally at their mercy? On the contrary, the Bible teaches that you are what you *think* you are rather than what society or circumstances make you.

The Reprogramming Process

Proverbs 23:7 states this astounding, simple truth: "As he [man] thinketh in his heart, so is he" (*KJV*). What you think you can do determines what you can do. If you are convinced that you can change, then you probably can.

Recently, a good friend of mine committed suicide. She was an excellent housekeeper, had an attractive figure and nice clothes. She was a very capable person but she had an image of herself as being inadequate and useless. She thought about herself in a way that wasn't true. Because of this "thought lie" she became so despondent she took her own life. Those of us who knew her tried to help her. We'd make sincere statements, trying to build up her self-esteem. But she couldn't accept compliments or honest, positive evaluation about her capabilities. She thought so deeply within herself in negative terms that she decided she didn't want to live. She limited not only her performance but the duration of her life.

Are you building your own set of limitations? Start right now to think of yourself as a "tryer." Of course you have limitations, but start thinking of yourself, in your heart, as a person who is willing to try. You *can* do what you think you can. You *can* perform the way you think you'll perform.

Today, pick one thing you've always wanted to do and try it! Stan the lifeguard tried, and made delicious homemade wheat bread. Frail little 98-pound Elaine, the secretary with perfectly manicured nails, tried, and changed a tire on the family station wagon.

You need to learn to channel your thought patterns. It may not be easy for you to think positively about yourself, especially if you are accustomed to thinking negatively. It is very easy to think bad thoughts. When we are faced with a choice, we generally think the worst. Actually, there are three ways to think about any situation. You can think pessimistically, looking at life from your own negative or erroneous perspective. You can think neutrally, which requires more objectivity than most of us possess. Or you can think optimistically, looking at life from God's perspective.

Since you are inclined to view life from the human, rather than the neutral or divine vantage point, you need to train yourself to think properly, to reconstruct the thought patterns that issue from your heart.

Left to yourself that would be an impossible task. Where would you start? How could you decide what you should or shouldn't think about? The only way you can actually change the quality and content of your thoughts is to follow the God-prescribed pattern recorded in Philippians 4:8, and think about whatever is *true, honest, just, pure, lovely* and *of good report.*

Why should you think on those specific things? What will the results be in your life if you do?

Thinking on what is true solves the problem of unreality in thought. All truth isn't pretty, but to be effective you must face reality. You must face the reality that life isn't easy; that it's full of injustice, unanswerable questions and hard work. You must face the fact of who and what you are.

Many women have what I call a Scarlett O'Hara complex. The spitfire heroine of *Gone with the Wind* lived her entire life running from reality. Whenever she faced a crisis or a problem she would just blank it out, refusing to think about it, pretending it didn't exist. Her standard approach to any dilemma was, "I won't think of it now." Scarlett O'Hara never faced reality and in the last paragraph of the final chapter of the book, after she has lost Rhett Butler, she still refuses to face the truth that he has gone. She says, "I'll think of it all tomorrow, at Tara. I can stand it then. Tomorrow, I'll think of some way to get him back. After all, tomorrow is another day."

Have you, like Scarlett, been running from reality? Think on what is true; face life and yourself as they are, not as you want them to be. My Aunt Carrie used to say, "No one ever turns off a water faucet unless they see it running." In other words, you can't conquer facts unless you face them.

A good self-image isn't based on dreams but truth. In the following space write one reality about yourself you've refused to face. One you want to conquer by admitting it exists and dealing with it.

Thinking on what is honest solves the poblem of dishonest thoughts. Are you lying to yourself about your life and your relationships? You cannot base your life on lies. You must be honest about situations and your part in them or you'll never face responsibility. You must be honest enough to admit that you'll be tempted to candy-coat and rationalize what you think, say and do; that you may manipulate situations and people.

If you have a poor self-image chances are that you're afraid to approach people openly and honestly. You don't want to be rejected or appear foolish. So, to protect yourself, you use subtle, less obvious means to get what you want. In that way you are dishonest with yourself and others.

Write one dishonest thought you are nurturing about yourself:

Thinking on what is just solves the problem of unfair thoughts. The basic problem with human judgments is that they are always based on incomplete and inaccurate information. There is no way anyone can judge with complete fairness and total objectivity. Yet, we are always ready to label, analyze and pronounce sentence on the faults and failures of ourselves and others. Frequently we don't do ourselves justice. We are unfair in the way we think about ourselves and as a result our self-esteem is damaged.

As an example, I've lived most of my life believing I am clumsy. I could write a book about my most embarrassing moments, all caused by my so-called clumsiness.

When I was in junior high I fell *up* the stairs in my first pair of high-heeled shoes. In senior high, when I was playing piano in the state music contest I missed the piano bench and landed on the floor. When I was eight months pregnant I fell flat on my abdomen when all I was doing was walking on the sidewalk to get to my car. I am famous for running into doors and walls, dropping things, breaking expensive dishes and being adorned with more bruises than a six-year-old.

A few months ago, a relative stranger pointed out to me that I'm not actually clumsy. I just move too fast. I'm always in too much of a hurry and my so-called clumsiness is actually a symptom of my impatience.

I remembered all the times George told me to slow down or to take it easy or not to try to carry so many things at once. Clumsy was such a convenient cover-up for my impatience, I merely accepted it. It was easier than changing my pace. But I'd been unfair to myself because ultimately, in thinking of myself as clumsy, I became what I decided I was.

Write one way you've thought unfairly about yourself in the last month:

Thinking on what is pure solves the problem of unholy thoughts. I was raised in the midwest and as a child I loved the snow. I could hardly wait until the first snowfall so I could make snow ice cream. Mama would always caution me to dig into the center of a sheltered drift so I would get clean snow. I noticed no matter how carefully I dug or how pure and crystal clear the dish of snow looked, when it melted there were tiny particles of dirt in the bottom of the bowl.

Our human thoughts are like that snow. No matter how pure we think they are, they are never totally without some particle of sin.

Scripture teaches that Almighty God alone is holy, totally without impurity. To think on what is pure you must concentrate on God. Psalm 99 repeatedly says, "He [God] is holy." First Peter 1:16 admonishes, "You shall be holy, for I [God] am holy." Christ said, in Matthew 5:8, that you will be happy if your heart is pure because then you will see God.

It isn't easy to think pure thoughts. The ways of the world bombard you externally and you battle your doubts, frustrations and desires internally. You will have to struggle to think the best, to think the good thought, to mentally dwell on the purity of a holy God. But when you do you will feel more positive about yourself.

Write one recurring, impure thought pattern you want to eliminate:

Thinking on what is lovely solves the problem of lingering thoughts. Many of us suffer from mental hangover. We become so absorbed in our grudges, worries and concerns that loveliness of thought is blotted out.

It may be a beautiful day—the sun shining, temperature pleasant. You have a wonderful evening to look forward to; you're going out to dinner at your favorite restaurant with your husband and close friends.

The kids just brought home good report cards. The car repair bill was less than you had expected it to be. You should be smiling, your heart should be singing. Those are lovely things.

But you can't seem to forget that dirty trick Mary played on you last week. Every time you think about it you get mad! You keep remembering how she manipulated to get the club to send her as the representative to the district convention when it was a foregone conclusion that you, as retiring president, would go.

Oh, you really didn't want to be gone for a week and conventions are usually dull, but it's the principle of the thing. Mary convinced the board she'd be doing you a favor by going. So she was sent instead of you. What gall! After you'd served two consecutive terms as president! She shouldn't be allowed to get away with it. There must be something you can do.

Whatever happened to that beautiful day? How ridiculous to let the pettiness of the past mar the loveliness of the moment. Whatsoever things are lovely—think on those things.

Write down your most prevalent, bothersome lingering thought:

Now write a lovely thought to displace it:

Thinking on what is of good report (what is virtuous and praiseworthy) solves the problem of passed-on thoughts. It is human nature to be quiet about the good and to voice the bad. We are slow to compliment but quick to complain. An old adage says, "Bad news travels fast"; another, "No news is good news." In other words, we remember and repeat the bad things far more readily and eagerly than the good.

When you hear a bad report—whether it's true or not—you dwell on it. When you hear a good report you probably experience a momentary surge of pleasure then drop it. Next time you're with a group, try stating nothing but good reports and see how hard it is. You'll have to concentrate on positives. Think of virtues rather than faults, praises instead of criticisms. Apply virtues and praises not only to others but to yourself. Filling in the following spaces will help you get started.

1. My greatest virtue is

2. The most positive quality I contribute to my marriage (or friendship) is

3. Today, one thing I did for which I deserve honest, realistic praise is

REMEMBER: IF YOU THINK YOU CAN, YOU CAN!

Workshop

Some of your heart attitudes are negative and some are positive. A negative heart attitude will bring about a series of negative responses in yourself and others, such as: (1) negative reaction from others; (2) a deepening negativism in yourself; (3) an improper relationship to God; (4) an effect on your actions, and (5) poor health.

The following is a list of the common, negative heart attitudes everyone has from time to time. Perhaps one of these is a consuming force in your life. This workshop will help you eliminate a negative attitude with a positive Scripture.

Read the list and put a check (✓) by eight of the heart problems that are most common to you. Write your definition of the word beneath it. Verify the meaning in a dictionary. Next, look up the Scripture verse, read it several times, savoring the intent, then write in your own words how you can use that verse to erase a negative idea. *Memorize the Scriptures.* From this time on, anytime a negative heart attitude surfaces, remove it by quoting and acting according to the Bible verse you have memorized.

Heart problem	*Scripture Solution*
1. Anger	Psalm 37:8
2. Anxiety	Philippians 4:6,7

3. Doubt   Matthew 21:21,22

4. Bitterness   Ephesians 4:30-32

5. Envy   Colossians 3:2

6. Fear   Psalm 34:4

7. Guilt   Romans 8:1

8. Irritability   Colossians 3:15-17

9. Impatience   James 1:2-4

10. Resentment   Romans 12:19

11. Selfishness   Romans 15:1-3

12. Depression   Matthew 5:4

13. Stubbornness   Proverbs 29:1

SELF-EXAMINATION: 3
A SPIRITUAL PHYSICAL

How well do you know yourself? That's a difficult question to answer. Remember Paul in Romans 12:3 said that you need to make a sane estimate of your capabilities. To do that, you must examine yourself, give yourself a "spiritual physical."

You've probably had several physical examinations during your lifetime. When you go to the doctor for your yearly physical you expect to be thoroughly checked. You wouldn't think you'd had a complete examination if all the doctor did was look in your ear, poke a tongue depressor in your mouth, ask you to say "ah," listen to your heart, slap you on the shoulder and say, "Nancy, you're in excellent health." A good doctor checks details and minor irregularities.

You need to take the same approach with your

45

spiritual health. You need to check periodically for minor irregularities in your attitudes and emotions to keep your soul and self-image in good condition. You should practice preventive medicine.

Evaluate Yourself

Many people settle comfortably into their habit patterns and seldom, if ever, evaluate what their life-style is like or what their motivations and goals are. Some get bored; they're in a rut. Others face constant turmoil, experiencing conflict with friends, neighbors, co-workers, family and within themselves. They know something is wrong but they never take that necessary step to correct the problem: they don't practice the art of self-examination.

There are two important reasons why you should evaluate yourself.

You need to get to know yourself. You may not know yourself as well as you think you do. You may be operating on misconceptions that you or others have programmed into you. As a result, you end up overestimating or underestimating your capabilities.

There's a very likable you somewhere in your life. If you haven't met her yet you're in for a pleasant experience. That's why self-examination is important. It helps you get to know yourself.

Self-examination forces you to keep yourself and others in proper perspective.

It is my personal opinion that a prime reason for the failure of so many marriages and the frustrations in so many parent-child relationships is a lack of self-examination. Nobody stays the same. We change daily. Sometimes we shrink, other times we grow, but you are a different person than you were 10 years ago, a month ago or even yesterday. Yet, most people run their lives oblivious to these changes, failing to recognize them. So they believe they are the same as they were when they were 20 years old, and that their husband or wife holds the same values and opinions he or she had when they got married.

They see their 17-year-old son, Tommy, as the same self-indulgent boy he was when he was six, although he has grown into an unselfish, giving person. Or they continue to stereotype their teenage daughter as a sweet and soft-hearted girl when actually she's become quite a cynic.

Without examination, relationships remain unbalanced or are destroyed. Self-evaluation reveals changes, flaws, strengths and failures. Internal diagnosis is as essential to your spiritual and emotional growth as good food, rest and exercise are to your physical well-being.

Getting to know yourself involves more than a brief, cursory glance. It requires meditation. Meditation is not, as some cults and eastern religions teach, blanking out. According to God's Word, it is deep, concentrated mental focusing on a certain set of facts. It is tuning-in. In Psalm 4:4 David said, "Meditate in your heart upon your bed, and be still."

This verse indicates that meditation is *the process* for examination; your heart—your emotions, will, intellect, conscience and sense of awareness—is *the object* of your search. *The method* is to set yourself apart from others, in a quiet place. You'll never discover what you need to know about yourself by pondering during the three-minute commercial on TV or by asking others.

Examine Your Relationship with God

God has instructed you to examine yourself. At the same time He is available to help you do it. First Corinthians 11:28 exhorts, "Let a man examine himself." Psalm 26:2 says, "Examine me, O Lord, and try me; test my mind and my heart." Are these statements contradictory? I see them as complementary. God never asks you to do anything without providing the way for you to accomplish it. You may tell your son to go to the store to buy milk, but you also give him your car to drive and the money to buy the milk. You gave the instruction but you also supplied the way for him to obey your request.

God instructs you to examine yourself, then enables you to do it. He will try you and, as He does, you can identify your strengths and weaknesses. He will test your heart and mind, much the same way a teacher grades an examination paper, checking what is right in you and what is wrong.

How well you understand yourself depends on your relationship with God. Proverbs 9:10 says, "The fear of the Lord is the beginning of wisdom, and the knowledge of the Holy One is understanding." *The Living Bible* paraphrases it this way: "For the reverence and fear of God are basic to all wisdom. Knowing God results in every other kind of understanding."

Write what you think the word "fear" means.

Two synonyms for fear are "awe" and "respect."

According to this verse if you want proper knowledge about yourself what do you do first? Write it down.

What should you look for as you examine yourself? How can you decide what factors to accept as positive contributors to a good self-image and which ones to reject as detractors?

Examine Your Relationship with Yourself

When I conduct a teacher training seminar I ask the trainees to list five definite strong points and their five most obvious weaknesses. People never have trouble stating their weaknesses but many can't list more than two strong points.

Furthermore, they frequently view as weaknesses characteristics that could just as easily be considered assets or could be overcome with a minimum of effort. Some "weaknesses" they've listed are: voice too loud, too organized, prefer people to programs, not enough education, would rather listen than talk and too soft-hearted.

The students who recorded these faults may have taken a precursory glance at their attributes but they had not examined themselves. As a result, they were subjectively unfair in judging themselves. They made a misdiagnosis based on surface facts and their self-worth suffered.

If your self-worth is suffering, a proper self-evaluation will evoke a healing process. As you examine yourself you will look for both positives and negatives and explore how to enhance the former and transform the latter.

Can you list five definite strong points and five obvious weaknesses about yourself?

Strengths

1.

49

2.
3.
4.
5.

Weaknesses
1.
2.
3.
4.
5.

Examine Your Life-style

Your life-style is the way you've chosen to live your life. The book of Proverbs says that righteous living will make you happy. Being righteous is acting in accordance with what is moral and acceptable by God's standards. Our society shuns that concept. Righteousness sounds so stuffy, so restrictive! Yet, Scripture teaches that "Blessings are on the head of the righteous" (Prov. 10:6).

If you are not living a righteous life your self-image is being adversely affected and you won't be completely happy. When you adhere to God's standards you develop a healthy sense of self-worth.

What are some specific requirements for a righteous life-style?

The first is to acknowledge the presence of unrighteousness. When you refuse to admit that parts of your life are impure, you can't change them; psychologists call this self-delusion. This kind of person "is pure in [her] own eyes, yet is not washed from [her] filthiness" (Prov. 30:12).

Doctors report that the greatest battle they wage

against cancer isn't in the operating room or in chemotherapy treatment, but in the patient's fear to admit she might have the disease. The patient ignores the symptoms and the malignancy goes untreated until it is incurable.

A friend of mine who is a nurse told me about a woman who accidentally bruised her chest. It didn't heal. It was irritated as her clothing rubbed against it. She developed an ugly bluish-red spot that eventually abscessed. Over two years after the accident, when the pain was so severe that it overcame her fears, she went to a doctor. The verdict: cancer that required radical surgery.

We all have heard similar stories about people who wouldn't acknowledge the presence of or refused to get treatment for cancer. Their unrealistic attitude didn't eliminate the malignancy; it merely prolonged their misery and made treatment of the malady difficult, drastic or impossible. Unrighteousness is a sinful cancer in your soul and refusing to face the reality of it doesn't eliminate it; it prolongs and intensifies the problems.

Another requirement for a righteous life-style is to remove unrighteousness. I recently bought a tube of squeeze-out, rub-in spot remover. George had a grease stain on a new necktie and asked me to try to get it out. The package directions said all I had to do was squeeze some solution onto the spot, rub it in, let it dry and brush it off. I was skeptical. It sounded so simple I was sure it wouldn't work but I followed the instructions and 20 minutes later the spot was gone.

It may seem equally impossible that, in two simple steps, you can start to remove an unacceptable behavior pattern from your life. But you can. All you have to do

51

is *confess* and *forsake* your unrighteous behavior (see Prov. 28:13). Confession isn't the complicated process you may think it is. Confession is admitting that unrighteousness exists and agreeing with God that what you're doing doesn't meet His standards for righteousness. You don't have to beg, cry, do penance or recite printed prayers. To forsake an improper life-style means you renounce it and abandon it.

Whatever you do about your life-style, the results are guaranteed, "He who conceals his transgressions will not prosper, but he who confesses and forsakes them will find compassion" (Prov. 28:13).

List several unacceptable behavior patterns you see in your life that you should confess and forsake.

Write at least one way you can immediately start to rechannel each of the patterns you listed.

Another requirement for achieving a righteous life-style is to practice righteousness. A righteous life-style abounds with good things and results in a good self-image.

If you care about yourself you will probably do what is best for you. You will live righteously, therefore you will reap what you sow. "Don't be under any illusion: you cannot make a fool of God! A man's harvest in life will depend entirely on what he sows. If he sows for his own lower nature his harvest will be the death and decay of his own nature. But if he sows for the Spirit he will reap the harvest of everlasting life by the Spirit" (Gal. 6:7,8, *Phillips*).

If you are not practicing righteousness it may be because you have a poor self-image. So you act out of accord with the moral, social and physical laws God has established. By catering to your lower instincts you "prove" to yourself and others that you are no good.

One of my best friends in high school was a beautiful girl. She came from a socially prominent family and had everything money could buy: her own car, lovely clothes and a generous allowance. Her parents pampered and idolized her; she was their most prized possession. She had the world on a string, except she slept with almost every boy who took her out; she drank profusely and attended every wild party that was thrown. She was rejected by the one boy she truly cared for. He called her a tramp.

When it happened, I hugged her and tried to console her but as she sat crying, she mumbled over and over, "He's right. I'm no good. I'm worthless. I'm just a worthless toy." Her immoral conduct was a cover-up, a misguided attempt to make her appear important and carefree; she was trying to compensate for her lack of self-respect. Practicing righteousness is a necessity if you are going to achieve a healthy, balanced self-image.

You should plant in your life the spiritual things that will yield a harvest of everlasting life. When you do you will reap the fruit of the Spirit and God will nurture within you these positive feelings of self-worth:

Love—You will learn to value yourself in the same way God does.

Joy—You will be happy and satisfied regardless of circumstances and conditions.

Peace—You will be secure and free from agitating passions that detract from your self-worth.

Patience—You will possess a calmness that allows for imperfections in yourself and others.

Kindness—You will feel useful and needed and be motivated to serve God and others.

Goodness—Your life will be stable and your defensiveness subdued.

Faithfulness—Your self-confidence will increase as you develop a stubborn, persistent reliance on God and as you realize what He can do in and through you.

Gentleness—You will manifest a tenderness in your thoughts and actions toward others and yourself.

Self-control—You will act with restraint and possess an equanimity that comes from mastering your passions rather than letting them master you.

All of these positives are available if you will examine yourself and sow for the Spirit. Isn't it worth a try?

REMEMBER: SELF-EXAMINATION IS ESSENTIAL FOR A BALANCED EXISTENCE.

Workshop

Read each statement carefully then rate yourself according to the following scale: A—always, U—usually, S—sometimes, N—never.

1. I need to know myself better ＿＿
2. I have respect for myself ＿＿
3. I am more aware of my weaknesses than I am of my strengths ＿＿
4. I understand why I do the things I do ＿＿

5. I am aware of some unrighteous patterns in my life that need to be altered ____
6. I am a contented person ____
7. Basically, I am secure ____
8. I am, in my opinion, a stable person ____
9. I am a perfectionist ____
10. I am easily influenced by circumstances or the opinions of others ____

4 IMAGE DETRACTORS

What have you discovered about yourself so far? Hopefully you've unearthed some factors that have been detracting from your self-image.

Did you find that you are locked into behaving in set patterns or thinking about yourself in a certain way, and that you are so accustomed to being like you are that you have accepted unacceptable habits with an attitude of, "That's just the way I am"?

Perhaps you've justified unrighteous feelings and attitudes by saying, "Everyone has her faults." Or, have you realized that you want to change, but you simply don't know how?

Maybe you've discovered that you're being conquered by your faults and problems because you are inadvertently trapped in them. You're so entangled in the situation that you can't see any possibilities for a solution. If so, you're being hampered by an image detractor called "tunnel vision."

Tunnel Vision

A person with tunnel vision looks in only one direction; she never notices peripheral areas or explores different avenues. For a woman with tunnel vision, the only way to reach the other end of a tunnel is to go straight through it. She'd never think of getting a ladder and climbing over the tunnel or scaling the mountain to the left or swimming across the river on the right or backtracking and taking a different route.

People with tunnel vision are dogmatic; they're the ones who tell you, "Don't bother me with facts; my mind is already made up." They believe there is only one way to do something or one way to act and they would rather suffer than change.

If you sincerely want to improve your self-image you can't have tunnel vision; you must practice *alternative thinking*. Alternative thinking is coming up with as many acceptable solutions as you possibly can; it is widening the scope of your approach.

Diane had to learn to think in alternatives. She was desperate when she came to ask my advice. Her father had died recently and Diane was frantic because she assumed her mother would have to come and live with her and Sam. Her mother is a fiery, independent, outspoken person and they had never gotten along too well. Diane felt smothered by her mother. I asked her why she had to allow her mother to move in.

"Well, because," she snapped.

"Why?" I asked again.

"Well, because dad is dead. She is my mother and we'd never consider letting her live alone."

"Why?" I asked again.

Frustrated, Diane argued with me for 10 minutes, defending why she was going to do something she felt was a mistake and that she didn't want to do. I said, "Then you're convinced there are no alternatives?"

She thought for a minute and shook her head. "I don't see any."

I suggested, just on the off chance there might be another solution, that we write down some possibilities, no matter how outlandish or farfetched they might seem. Here is the list we came up with in just a few minutes:

1. Talk to mother; get her ideas.
2. Talk to Sam; get his ideas.
3. Let mother live alone.
4. Let her rent a room in her house to a boarder.
5. Hire a live-in housekeeper.
6. Have her move to a retirement community.
7. Live with her son and his family.
8. Have her move in with us.
9. Send her on a cruise to find a husband.
10. Offer to help her financially but tell her it would be best if she didn't live with us.
11. Let her decide what she wants to do and help her any way we can.

Diane realized she wasn't trapped and after talking with her mother they reached a mutually satisfactory solution; alternatives 1,2,5 and 10 were used, plus her mother got a part-time job as a children's librarian.

Diane thought she was trapped but she wasn't. You aren't either. There are alternatives if you seek them. If you want to be a capable person who can attack and solve problems, you must shed the image detractor of tunnel vision.

Emotions: Who's in Control?

Your emotional reactions can also be an image detractor. Uncontrolled emotions are never pleasant to see or experience. It's hard to appreciate or enjoy anyone who easily flies off the handle, who laughs too loudly, talks incessantly or cries too easily. You can be embarrassed for and by them.

You are an emotional being who experiences pain and pleasure and the way that you handle your emotional reactions can enhance or devalue your self-image. If you let your emotions control you rather than your controlling them, you won't feel as good about yourself as you should.

Proverbs 25:28 says that a woman who has no control over her spirit is "like a city that is broken into and without walls."

I've seen what can happen in a city that is "broken into and without walls." In 1956 a tornado wiped out half of my hometown in Kansas. Within minutes after the disaster struck, looters descended like vultures; trampling possessions, rummaging in the ruins, robbing even the unburied dead. People whose homes had been damaged or destroyed were vulnerable to most outside forces. There were no doors to keep out the looters; no roofs to keep out the rainstorm that followed; no place to go for relief. They were totally at the mercy of nature and their fellowman; helpless, unprotected, unable to control what was happening. Utter chaos reigned until martial law was declared.

If your emotions rule you, if you have no control over your spirit, your life is like that city. You are vulnerable to every incident, every criticism, every person you meet.

Do you control your emotions or are you letting them control you? List two emotions that frequently get the best of you; then, beside each one, list how you act when you are being controlled by them. For example, if you lose your temper a lot you would list anger as the emotion and the symptoms might be slamming doors, yelling and kicking the dog.

Emotion   *Symptoms*

1.

2.

Speak No Evil

Another image detractor is your speech. Do you alienate people because you don't control your tongue? What you say, why and how you say it not only causes others to reject you but can make you dislike yourself. Examine yourself to see what unrighteous speech habits may be inadvertently contributing to your self-devaluation.

Perhaps you talk too much. If you do, eventually

you're going to say the wrong thing or be misunderstood. Quantity of speech affects the quality. Proverbs 10:19 says: "When there are many words, transgression is unavoidable, but he who restrains his lips is wise."

When faced with a choice of speaking or keeping silent, which do you do? If you're inclined to speak but aren't sure whether you should or not, it's wise not to. When in doubt, don't. After all, "Even a fool, when he keeps silent, is considered wise" (Prov. 17:28).

Knowing when to say something is important. Proper timing adds richness and dimension to conversation. "Like apples of gold in settings of silver is a word spoken in right circumstances" (Prov. 25:11).

I was absolutely devastated a few years ago when I ran over my fat, beautiful chocolate-point Siamese cat as I was pulling into the driveway. And I dreaded telling my friend Ruth, who had given him to me, what had happened. She'd trusted me to take good care of him and asked about his well-being every time I saw her. Coward that I am, I waited until she asked how he was. Then, with a lump in my throat, I told her about the horrendous happening. Without blinking an eye she hugged me and said, "Well, he was happy, loved and had a good home when he was alive; what more can any of us ask?" Her words were truly apples of gold.

God's ideal is cautious speech: words graciously spoken, well-timed and wisely understated.

You also want your speech to be positive, pleasant and cheerful. Are you a verbal pessimist? Or perhaps you have an uncanny knack for saying the wrong thing at the worst possible moment? Proverbs 12:25 says, "Anxiety in the heart . . . weighs it down, but a good word makes it glad."

61

Does your speech build up others or tear them down? If you practice speaking a "good word" you'll have a positive effect in their lives and will think more highly of yourself. What is a good word? It's saying what will encourage rather than what will cause anxiety. God's standard for quality of speech is to speak what enriches and edifies, consoles and uplifts.

Controlling your tongue means you must watch both what you say and how you say it. Being caustic or abrupt doesn't endear you to anyone. "A gentle answer turns away wrath, but a harsh word stirs up anger" (Prov. 15:1).

Do you give gentle answers or are you apt to make harsh replies? Part of God's standard for righteous speech is gentleness: saying what is refined, courteous, kind and generous.

To evaluate your gentleness factor, write down what your standard reply would be in each of these situations:
1. Your child asks you to read to him when you're busy.

2. You get out of the shower to answer the telephone and an insurance salesman who is canvassing the neighborhood is calling.

3. Someone accuses you of saying something you didn't say or of doing something you didn't do.

4. Someone fairly and objectively criticizes you but you don't want to hear what was said.

5. Someone vehemently and loudly disagrees with you, and you know you're right.

6. Someone accidentally spills something sticky on your best dress and immediately apologizes.

Another problem is hasty speech. Do you just blurt out whatever happens to be on your mind or do you think about what you're going to say? Do you think about how it will affect whoever hears it? "The heart of the righteous ponders how to answer, but the mouth of the wicked pours out evil things" (Prov. 15:28).

Before you say something do you sift your reply through your mind, to see if it's the smart thing to say; through your conscience, to see if it's the edifying thing to say; through your will to see if it needs to be said at all, and through your concern to see if it's the appropriate thing to say? That's how a righteous woman ponders her words in her heart.

The opposite of pondering is pouring. During lunch the other day I shook the pepper shaker, expecting a few grains to fall onto my food. Instead, the entire shaker-full of pepper tumbled into my salad. Needless to say, the food was ruined. The manager surmised that playful teenagers had purposely loosened the cap.

Poured words are like poured pepper—carefully sifted speech seasons your life but used indiscriminately words can ruin what is otherwise a good thing. God's standard is pondered speech, thoughtful words that season rather than destroy.

Selfishness: The Ugly I

Selfishness is another image detractor that destroys your feelings of self-worth because it alienates you from the concern of others, breaks contact with them and destroys compassion for them. You get all wrapped up in "The Ugly I."

When I taught sixth grade I had my class write definitions for words I called "human hurters." One boy turned in the best definition of selfishness I've ever heard. He said, "Selfishness is wanting my own way no matter if it is best for me or will hurt someone else. It is keeping what I don't need just so I won't have to share it."

What, in your opinion, is selfishness?

Write three antonyms for selfishness:
1.
2.
3.

Are you selfish? Selfishness has many symptoms. They may appear isolated or in combination with one another. Some are:
1. *Defensiveness*—because you must prove to everyone that you are right.

2. *Guilt*—because you aren't willing to share when you know you could and should.
3. *Fear*—you won't get what you want or you'll lose what you have.
4. *Envy and jealousy*—because you want to be the center of attention and you dislike anything or anyone that detracts from your glory or interferes with your plans.
5. *Unkindness*—because a selfish person is automatically insensitive. You focus on what you can do *for* yourself but never notice what you do *to* others.
6. *Impatience*—because you want your own way and instant gratification.

Are you manifesting any of these symptoms? I have a problem with impatience. I actually use "rush" terms like "hurry" or "come on." Or, when we're riding in the car I inevitably try to tell George what I think the fastest route is, then I expect him to follow it! Frequently, I hear myself asking, "Why are you taking so long?"

My personal goal for myself this year is to slow down. I force myself not to comment when I'm waiting for someone. I am pledged not to say one word to George about which streets to take. When I start to get that irritating, slightly elevated, impatient tone in my voice, I stop, take a deep breath, and reflect on what's in my heart at that moment. Do you know what I discover always lurking there? *Selfishness!* I want life run on my time schedule. My heart is so full of selfishness I get impatient with anything or anyone who interferes with my pace. So I made up this motto to repeat to myself whenever I start to use "rush" terms: Impatience is actually my selfishness imposed on others. What difference will 10 seconds make tomorrow?

My motto has two purposes. The first statement forces me to acknowledge my problem and the second puts things into perspective.

Why don't you pick one selfishness symptom that is most bothersome to you and write it here.

Now, write three concrete, positive things you can do to counter it.

1.

2.

3.

Now, make up a motto to counter the negative overflow.

A practical way to counter selfishness is to plan every day to do one special thing for each person with whom you come in contact. Think in terms of what you can do for them. What can you do for your husband the first thing in the morning to help his day get off to a good start? What can you say to the service station attendant to cheer his day, as he is moving so slowly when you're in such a hurry? What can you do for your boss, your hairdresser, the grocery clerk or your child or roommate to help them and make life easier for them?

All of us are selfish sometimes. But if selfishness is a pattern in your life you won't be satisfied or happy because one of the greatest pleasures in life comes from giving of yourself to others. As you conquer "The Ugly I" you will start feeling more positive about yourself.

REMEMBER: YOU CAN CHANGE! IMAGE DETRACTORS ARE ERASABLE.

Workshop

This workshop is designed to help you diagnose your attitudes, actions and emotions. First, read each sentence and fill in the blank with the letter of the word that best describes you (A—always; U—usually; S—sometimes; N—never). When you've finished, read each sentence to someone you know quite well and ask them to tell you which word they would use to accurately describe what you're like. You may want to consult several friends and family members. If there are obvious discrepancies between how you and the other persons answer, you should take a closer look at your relationships.

1. I am dogmatic ____
2. I graciously accept criticism ____
3. I think how something will affect me before I think how it will affect others ____
4. I am polite and courteous to others ____
5. I have a tendency to snap back when someone says something with which I disagree ____
6. I have a temper ____
7. I compliment more than I criticize ____
8. I talk too much ____
9. When I am right I want others to acknowledge that I am ____
10. I am generous with my time and possessions ____
11. I am optimistic ____
12. I openly speak my mind ____
13. I frequently raise my voice ____
14. I am a patient person ____

15. I am quick to condemn ____
16. I am an easy-going person ____
17. Little things greatly upset me ____
18. I have a good memory ____
19. I think before I act or speak ____
20. It is difficult for me to say I'm sorry ____
21. I believe a person should apologize only if she is at fault in a situation ____
22. I prefer to keep my feelings to myself ____
23. I get upset if my plans are disrupted ____
24. I can tell what the people closest to me need without their asking ____
25. I am defensive ____

HOW 5
TO AGAPE
YOURSELF

Margie is a petite, vivacious young woman who has a poor self-image. One day, after I'd finished teaching a Bible lesson about examining and eliminating negatives she came to me and said, "You know, Mrs. Berry, I'm doing what we've talked about but even with the negatives gone I still don't feel good about myself. I don't like myself. I find it is very hard to accept the positives I've discovered."

Perhaps that's a problem you face. You've been able to isolate some problems and take some steps toward improving your behavior and attitudes but you still can't accept or appreciate yourself. You need to learn to love yourself.

What does the idea of self-love conjure up in your thinking? Ego? Pride? Selfishness? The idea of someone bragging and patting herself on the back? Certainly, those are negative facets of self-love; but there is a healthy, necessary form of self-love that each of you needs in order to develop a positive sense of self-esteem.

Today, the cultural misuse of the word love has deteriorated the meaning and reduced it to trivia. I decided to record all of the times in a 48-hour period that someone said, "I love." Here is what I heard:

"I love bagels."
"I love hot-fudge sundaes."
"I love that pantsuit."
"I love my cat."
"I love these new trash bags."
"I love this weather."
"I love having stereo in my car."
"I love the snow."
"I love baseball best."
"I love you, Mommy."
"I love this popcorn."
"I love his singing."
"I love your dress."
"I love you."
"I love mustard on hamburgers."
"I love ketchup."

Somehow, this overusage detracts from the precious concept of love, rendering it common, making it seem mediocre. This watering-down in intensity and meaning is reflected in the dictionary definition. A 1970 Webster's dictionary defines love as "a deep and strong feeling of attachment; great affection." Whereas one from the forties says love is "a merciful attitude toward someone." Love has, in our thinking, degenerated from serving to feeling.

Write your definition of love.

Four Kinds of Love

The Greeks, during the time of Alexander the Great, devised the best language system in history for differentiating the meaning of words. They had four separate words to define love. A brief study of their terms will help you understand a word that to you may mean as little as a fluttering heart or as much as willingness to die for a noble cause.

The first word that Greeks used to categorize love was eros. From it we get the word "erotic." *Eros* is romantic, sensual love; it is passion. *Eros* is a selfish love—it always seeks some kind of physical gratification.

The second kind of love the Greeks defined is stergo. *Stergo* is instinctive love such as a mother has for her young. It is part of the human mechanism, a natural inclination to support or oblige because of a relationship. You see *stergo* in action in family relationships (the old blood-is-thicker-than-water reaction), in patriotism (loving and being willing to sacrifice for the national good) and between pets and their masters.

The third kind of love is phileo. This is brotherly love; man's humanly inspired love for man. *Phileo* is a higher form of love than *eros* or *stergo* because it is rooted in a mutual attraction between the person who is doing the loving and the person who receives it.

Phileo is the "liking" that is necessary in friendships, families and marriages to help them survive the ups and downs of the relationship. It's enjoying someone's company and treating them with respect.

The fourth Greek word, agape, expresses love in its highest form. Agape love generates totally out of a sense of value for the person being loved. It never says, "I love you because," but simply, "I love you." It is unconditional and unearned. *Agape* never seeks anything in return and is motivated by a sacrificial need to give, not get. *Agape* is the kind of love God has for man, based on His grace, His unmerited favor and His charitable attitude.

Agape Love

Agape love is a value, not an emotion. Emotional love is as inconsistent as our feelings are. For example, I *agape* my child—I value him simply because he exists. I may become angry with him or be disappointed in him or pleased with him; therefore I express different emotions toward him at different times. But my *agape* love —the value I place on that child—never wavers.

Love is not something you feel but something you do. W.E. Vine said, "Love can be known only from the actions it prompts."[1] In other words, *agape* love always acts as if the receiver is of infinite value.

As applied to self-love, *agape* means you must learn to value yourself. Jesus Christ taught the principle of self-love. " 'You shall love the Lord your God with all your heart, and with all your soul, and with all your mind.' This is the great and foremost commandment. And a second is like it, 'You shall love your neighbor as yourself' " (Matt. 22:37-39).

Read these verses again then complete the sentence to show how our love priorities are to be established.

1. First you shall love
2. Then you shall love
3. As a result, you can love

" 'You shall love the Lord your God with all your heart, and with all your soul, and with all your mind.' This is the great and foremost commandment." Before you can adequately and fruitfully love anyone else you must first love God because your relationship with Him is the basis for all other human relationships. It establishes the love cycle.

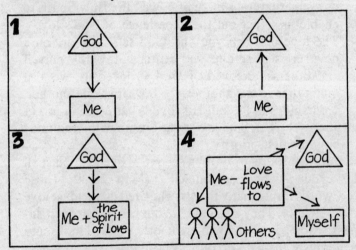

1. God sets our love in motion with His love. "We love, *because* He first loved us" (1 John 4:19, italics added.). There is, of course, a quality of human love —a combination of *eros, stergo* and *phileo*—that people apart from God experience. But it has neither the depth, richness nor redeeming grace of God's love. God's essence is love, so He and He alone can initiate *agape* love within us.

73

2. Man responds by accepting God's love and returning it. Man values God in return for God's valuing him. "And we have come to know and have believed the love which God has for us. God is love, and the one who abides in love abides in God, and God abides in him" (1 John 4:16).

3. The Holy Spirit enables this love cycle. "By this we know that we abide in Him and He in us, because He has given us of His Spirit" (1 John 4:13). God's love can't be generated through a human agent so He sent us a supernatural source of power, the Holy Spirit, to enable us to act out the experience of God's love.

4. The love between you and God sets into motion a new series of actions and attitudes toward yourself and others. "Beloved, if God so loved us, we also ought to love one another. . . . If we love one another, God abides in us, and His love is perfected in us" (1 John 4:11,12). So a love relationship with God must be your first priority.

But then we read, "And a second is like it, 'You shall love your neighbor as yourself' " (Matt. 22:39). Those few words imply many things. They tell us we must love our neighbor. They also indicate our bent toward selfishness. Most of us tend to treat others less kindly and generously than we do ourselves. We see this in young children; the first one in line always picks the biggest piece of chocolate cake. Adults are more subtle but they are inclined to take the best for themselves; they question someone else's motives instead of their own; they do whatever will be the most convenient for them.

The *Amplified Bible* says, "You shall love your neighbor as [you do] yourself." Not only is that a command to counter selfishness but it can also be taken as a simple statement of fact: You're going to love others in the same way you love yourself. You'll treat them the way you treat yourself. If you're insecure you'll have trouble trusting others. If you're unduly critical of yourself you'll find you're also judgmental and critical of others. If you reject yourself and fail to recognize your individual worth you'll reject others as well.

If you don't love yourself you can't love anyone else. You are supposed to love yourself in the same way God loves you, to *agape* yourself. How can you, in a practical way, do that?

Acknowledge your worth. Realize that you are of infinite value to God, yourself and others. There is a marked difference between being unworthy and being worthless. You may be unworthy in the sense that you are undeserving of God's grace and the blessings He bestows, but you aren't worthless!

You are so valuable to Almighty God that He sacrificed His most precious Son to save you. "For God so greatly loved and dearly prized [*you*] that He [even] gave up His only-begotten (unique) Son, so that [if *you* believe] in, [trust, cling to and rely on] Him [*you*] shall not perish—come to destruction, be lost—but have eternal (everlasting) life" (see John 3:16, *AMP*).

You are important to God. You are of value to Him, therefore you must be of value to yourself and others.

Remember, God created you and He never does anything worthless. Everything God does has permanent, lasting, eternal value. Receiving God's *agape* love gives you a sense of value in yourself, not because of what you are or can do in your humanity but because you realize how deeply God cares for you.

Sacrifice "I" for "U". Agape love is sacrificial so it

focuses on what is best for you, not merely on what you want. Often you want what isn't good for you. You want to lie around watching television when you should be exercising. You want the piece of chocolate cake you shouldn't eat or the vacation you can't afford. But if you truly love and value yourself in the same way God loves you, you will sacrifice certain things that you want in lieu of what is best for you.

List some activities, habits or attitudes you need to sacrifice for your own good:

Agape love is motivated by what you can give *of* yourself, *to* yourself, to make you what God knows you can be. *Agape* love sacrificially develops self-worth. When your will conflicts with God's desire and concern for your life, you relinquish what you like or want and give free flow to His direction. You don't do what is expedient for the moment to draw favorable attention to yourself, or what is comfortable in the situation. Rather you do God's will, which in the long run will be personally beneficial and permanently uplifting.

I am amazed at how many people are afraid to surrender to God in this way. They don't want to sacrifice what they have for something infinitely better. Contrary to popular belief, God isn't some holy dictator who, when we place our trust in Him, fences us in, takes away all of our pleasures then makes us do penance for the past.

The truth is, when we surrender to God we receive two things: grace and mercy. He gives us a lot of wonderful things we haven't earned and He doesn't give us the punishment we deserve. God's love accentuates the positive and eliminates the negatives so that you can stop doing what detracts or drags you down and creatively respond to yourself in ways that will enhance your self-image.

Relinquish reasons. Agape love is unconditional and unearned, so you do not have to wonder *why* you should like yourself or *what* you can do that will make you like yourself better. You accept yourself on God's basis and not on your own terms. You don't have to say, "I like myself because ... " Because I'm popular or dress well or live in a nice house or am an important executive or have a great sense of humor or because I'm Italian or English or my daddy served in the war. You love yourself for one reason—because God loves you. You simply say, "I like myself because God does." The only thing that can quench the development of a proper self-love is your refusal to bestow it upon yourself.

The Bible emphasizes the importance of loving— placing proper value on God, yourself and your fellow-man—as opposed to receiving love. The ultimate test of love is seen in how you use it.

Jesus didn't say, "Stand around feeling emotional about yourself and others and try to make someone love you." He said, "A new commandment I give to you, that you love one another, even as I have loved you, that you also love one another" (John 13:34).

The entire earthly ministry of Jesus Christ illustrates that love is not primarily a feeling for oneself or others but is acting out a different attitude toward yourself and those around you, one that says, "You are. Therefore you are of value."

Are You Ready to Agape Yourself?

First Corinthians 13 is called "The Love Chapter." Theologians, scholars, psychiatrists and psychologists consider it a complete picture of mature love. Since it is a portrait of God's love, although it describes how God loves us and how we should love others, it can also be applied to your relationship with yourself. Here are the essential attitudes and values for proper self-love.

Love suffereth long. Long-suffering is an old English term that means "to bear long." It denotes patience. You are unrealistic if you expect instantaneous results. Satisfactory development takes time. Growth is a gradual thing. Seeds don't sprout the day after they're planted. Infants don't become adults overnight. Growing up is tedious and also painful. Most parents have made at least one visit to the emergency room with their children. There are tears to cry, disappointments to face and dreams that die.

Be willing to suffer long with yourself as you grow and develop. Do you value yourself enough to be patient with yourself; to allow for imperfections and mistakes without feeling guilty, defeated or worthless?

Love is kind. Kindness is doing what is beneficial, being useful in a constructive way. We often misunderstand kindness. We think of it as doing something nice that will have pleasant results. That isn't necessarily true. It is doing, in a positive way, what needs to be done.

For example, one of my cats had a viral eye infection. Her eyes were swollen and the fur around them was

78

matted. So, to be kind, I took her to the vet. He gave her a shot and told me to put medicine in her eyes three times a day for one week. Poor Tabby didn't view my efforts as kindness. She howled, growled and stiffened when I put the medicine in her eyes. It was unpleasant for her. I'm sure she thought I had turned into a fiend who ran around attacking helpless house pets. But I was being kind and ultimately she reaped the benefits because I did what was best for her.

Do you value yourself enough to do things that are best for you; that build you up rather than tear you down; that are self-beneficial instead of self-gratifying?

Love envieth not. Whether you like it or not, you are who you are and that's never going to change. Wishing you could be like someone else or that you could be something you aren't only makes you more dissatisfied with yourself as a person.

When I was a little girl my friends and I used to play a game called "pretend you have different parents." I didn't want any parents except my own and I felt terribly disloyal and guilty whenever we'd play, but I enjoyed pretending my favorite movie stars were my mother and father.

I'd get so caught up in the game I would actually become dissatisfied with my own parents because I'd been pretending to be something I wasn't and I got a bad case of the envies.

Many adults get trapped in similar childish, make-believe games and end up dissatisfied with their lives. Do you value yourself enough to know and accept yourself for what you are, not what you—and perhaps others —wish you were?

Love vaunteth not itself. If you honestly love yourself

in the right way you won't brag, boast or promote yourself. You'll maintain a proper perspective about yourself, your position and your needs and be more concerned about others than you are about selling yourself. You will "do nothing from selfishness or empty conceit, but with humility of mind you will regard others as more important than yourself and not merely look out for your own personal interests, but also for the interests of others" (see Phil. 2:3,4). Do you value yourself enough to see yourself in perspective and relate in a giving way to others?

Love is not puffed up. The term "puffed up" in the original Greek language means to inflate the lungs in breathing. A modern colloquialism would be, love is not full of hot air.

Are you sincere, not taken with your own importance, or are you solicitous of people who can be useful to you because of their reputation or position? Do you act the same toward a salesclerk as you do toward an important executive from your business firm? Or do you put on airs?

Do you value yourself enough to have a settled, calm, realistic sense of self-acceptance, to just be yourself?

Love does not behave itself unseemly. To behave unseemly means you act in a way that will bring shame to you. Its opposite is being polite. Do you practice good manners, saying please, thank you, excuse me, and listening rather than interrupting when someone else is talking?

Pushy, domineering people usually brutalize others with rudeness because they have a low opinion of themselves, so they feel they need to fight for what they think is rightfully theirs. They can't relax in the normal course of events, consequently they often act shamefully.

Do you value yourself enough to conduct yourself so you can take personal pride in your actions and opinions?

Love seeketh not her own. Have you ever watched what a small child does when a playmate takes one of his favorite toys? He grabs, hits, cries, kicks or pinches to get it back. Frequently the only reason he wants the toy is because someone else has it. He selfishly demands his own way or rights for no good reason.

Are you like that child, seeking your own instead of God's best? Do you value yourself enough to want what God wants for your life instead of what you want or think you should have?

Love is not provoked. Being provoked is being greatly excited or agitated. Its opposite is having a good disposition, rolling with the punches and expecting less than perfection from the human you. If you love yourself in the right way you'll be at peace with, and be able to laugh at, yourself. Do you value yourself enough to relax and enjoy life?

Love thinketh no evil. Agape love doesn't hold grudges or dwell on past unpleasantness. It forgives and forgets and gives itself the benefit of a doubt. "[God] has not dealt with us according to our sins, nor rewarded us according to our iniquities . . . . As far as the east is from the west, so far has He removed our transgressions from us" (Ps. 103:10,12).

If God is willing to approach you fairly and compassionately, shouldn't you be willing to do the same for yourself and not deal with yourself according to your past blunders, errors and failings, but to drop them and start anew? Do you value yourself enough to confess, then forget; to learn from your mistakes rather than linger over them?

Love rejoiceth not in iniquity but rejoiceth in truth. Sometimes you may do the wrong thing to accomplish what you think is proper or necessary. Yet, when you reach your goal or get what you want you aren't satisfied. Something's missing. That's because the end didn't justify the means and if you're a normal person with an average conscience you find it hard to rejoice in iniquity.

Loving yourself means you care enough about yourself to try to do what's right and to change your approach if you're doing certain things you know are wrong. Do you value yourself enough to be happy when you do what's right and to be displeased enough with yourself to take corrective action when you do something wrong?

Love beareth all things. I found it extremely interesting, as I studied this concept, that bearing all things means "to cover closely." It implies sheltering and protecting the object that is valued.

I was reminded of a teacher I knew many years ago who thought so little of herself that she constantly exposed the worst about herself. She droned on about how her husband neglected her and what a boring companion and poor father he was. She told uncomplimentary stories about her children and described in detail their disrespectful attitudes, bad grades and belligerent attitude toward her. And she seemed to actually enjoy exalting her faults to anyone who'd listen. She didn't know how to "bear up," to keep quiet about the bad and stress the good.

First Peter 4:8 admonishes you, "Above all, keep fervent in your love for one another, because love covers a multitude of sins." If you have a good self-image you can adjust to and modify your faults instead of inflicting them on everyone. Do you value yourself enough to put your best foot forward, to "cover closely" your shortcomings and inadequacies rather than exposing them to others?

Love believeth all things. All love relationships must be based in trust. Do you have faith in yourself? Can you say with the apostle Paul, in Philippians 4:13, "I can do all things through Him who strengthens me"? Do you value yourself enough to trust yourself, being willing to use the natural talents and spiritual gifts God has given you?

Love hopeth all things. I once heard hope defined as expecting the best when you know the worst. Hope isn't grounded in the fact of what is, but in the possibility of what can and should be. "Hope that is seen is not hope; for why does one also hope for what he sees?" (Rom. 8:24).

Are you hopeful about yourself, striving to become what you can and should be? Do you value yourself enough to expect the best of yourself; to know you can accomplish something purposeful and to demand better of yourself in the future?

Love endureth all things. The kind of endurance spoken of here is an undergirding support. It means you don't cave in or give up on yourself. You have staying power; defeat isn't a word in your dictionary. In spite of past failures or bad circumstances or what appear to be insurmountable odds, you keep on keeping on. Do you value yourself enough to stand up for what you are and can be, to never cave in on yourself but to support yourself until you've seen a situation through to the finish?

Do you love yourself the way God *agapes* you? If you do, you're on the way to developing a good self-image.

REMEMBER: THE ONLY THING THAT CAN QUENCH THE DEVELOPMENT OF A PROPER SELF-IMAGE IS YOUR REFUSAL TO BESTOW IT ON YOURSELF.

Workshop

Since love is something you do, rate yourself below to see how well you are practicing positive self-love. Use the following scale: A—always; O—often; S—sometimes; N—never. Pick several areas where you can improve and work on them.

1. I eat healthy foods ____
2. I exercise ____
3. I have regular physical checkups ____
4. I get enough sleep and rest ____
5. I purposely pursue new interests and activities ____
6. I can laugh at my mistakes ____
7. I'm glad I'm me ____
8. I don't want to be like anyone else, just the best I can be ____
9. I have confidence in my capabilities ____
10. I know what my talents are and I use them to the fullest ____
11. I do not worry ____
12. I am generally polite and thoughtful of others ____
13. I have fun doing whatever I'm doing ____
14. I try to make restitution when I offend or hurt someone ____
15. I try not to impose my shortcomings on others ____

16. I have faith in myself ____
17. I want to improve myself wherever improvement is needed ____
18. I complete something if I start it ____
19. I have a positive attitude about myself ____
20. I *agape* myself ____

Note

1. W.E. Vine, *The Expository Dictionary of New Testament Words* (Old Tappan, N.J.: Fleming H. Revell, 1966), 4:21.

6 NOBODY'S PERFECT

No one is perfect! Say it aloud. No one is perfect. Your parents are not perfect. Neither is your employer, professor, husband, child or pastor. *You* are not perfect so you must be flexible in your approach to yourself. But how can you acknowledge all of your obvious imperfections and shortcomings and still maintain a good self-image?

The answer is found in Colossians 3:10: "You have finished with the old [person] and all [she] did and have begun life as a new [person], who is out to learn what [she] ought to be, according to the plan of God," (*Phillips*). Stop dwelling on what you are and concentrate on learning what you ought to be.

What an exciting concept! Right at this moment, no matter where you are or what's happened to you in the past, God is handing you a new lease on life. Whether you have been a Christian for many years or have never committed your life to Christ, this can be the starting point where you forget about your old self and begin life in Christ as a new you. From this moment on you don't ever again have to be hung up on what *used* to be if you commit yourself to learning what you *ought* to be.

Failure is an intrinsic component of any learning process. Bishop William Connor Magee said, "The man who makes no mistakes does not usually make anything!" Be flexible enough to allow for failure; it's part of growth.

What is flexibility? I define it this way: flexibility is relinquishing the old for the new as needed. It is being finished with your old self and all you did and beginning life as a new person who is out to learn what you ought to be according to the plan of God.

One of the things I treasure most about my relationship with Christ is that it has given me the freedom to fail. As long as I'm doing my best, the results of my efforts are God's responsibility, not mine.

Actually, what we call failure is simply having circumstances turn out differently than we had predetermined they should. You have not failed if you've attempted something and didn't achieve the results you expected. The greatest failure in life is never to have tried at all.

All of us struggle with our imperfections and failures. When Christians list great men of God, one of the first who comes to mind is the apostle Paul. He is sometimes called the apostle's apostle. Before his conversion he vehemently persecuted and was instrumental in the deaths of many Christians.

After his conversion he boldly erased the past and sought to convert not only Gentiles but the very Jews he had led in attacks against the Christians. He became a mighty servant of the living God.

Yet, even Paul was overcome at times by his weaknesses and faults. In Romans 7:18-25 he poignantly pens his frustration with his imperfection. He cries out against it, loathing it, distraught by it. But in the depths of despair Paul realizes his potential and the flexibility that freedom in Christ has given him. Paul anguishes, "I know I am rotten through and through so far as my old sinful nature is concerned. No matter which way I turn I can't make myself do right. I want to but I can't!" (Have you ever felt that way about yourself, that no matter what you do, it's wrong?)

"When I want to do good, I don't; and when I try not to do wrong, I do it anyway." (Remember, this is Paul, the spiritual giant who is speaking, not you or me.) "Now, if I am doing what I don't want to, it is plain where the trouble is: sin still has me in its evil grasp.

"It seems to be a fact of life that when I want to do what is right, I inevitably do what is wrong. I love to do God's will so far as my new nature is concerned; but there is something else deep within me, in my lower nature, that is at war with my mind and wins the fight and makes me a slave to the sin that is still within me. In my mind I want to be God's willing servant but instead I find myself still enslaved to sin.

"So you see how it is: my new life tells me to do right, but the old nature that is still inside me loves to sin. Oh, what a terrible predicament I'm in!" (How disheartening it would be if he'd stopped there, because that's where many people are—in a terrible predicament because of their sin. But he continues), "Who will free me from my slavery to this deadly lower nature?" (And how sad if he ended with that question because it's one some of you may be asking. You've seen what you are but how can you change?) "Thank God! It has been done by Jesus Christ our Lord. *He* has set me free!" *(TLB)*.

Christ can also set *you* free! Free—to fail and to fall, to succeed and to be flexible toward yourself.

Unrealistic Demands

Most people are quite rigid in what they expect of themselves. They make unrealistic demands of themselves and act as if the word impossible isn't part of the English language.

Are you too hard on yourself or are you flexible as to what you pursue and hope to attain? Are your goals realistic?

There are two reasons why people set unrealistic goals: They overestimate their capabilities and set them too high or they sell themselves short and don't set their sights high enough. Neither is realistic. Flexibility toward goals means you are working toward something you believe God is enabling you to do. In most instances, you will be successful.

There are two kinds of goals: immediate and long-range. If your long-range goal is to be an English teacher your short-range goals must be to study hard, read a lot, and get a proper education.

Once you become a teacher, your short-range goal may be to teach the best eighth-grade English classes in the school and your long-range goal might be to get a Ph.D. in your field. That also involves a short-term goal of going further in school and getting a master's degree.

An interim goal could be that you want to write a book about the modern melodrama in paperback romances as part of your thesis. Once you get your Ph.D. you may set a goal to discard teaching entirely and become a lecturer and author. And someday you plan to win the Nobel Prize in literature.

The point is, goals change. So do desires. What is a long-range goal now may become an immediate one in the near future. Or you may want to discard certain goals in lieu of others. Setting realistic goals demands flexibility.

What are your goals? First, list three things you want to accomplish tomorrow, your immediate goals.
1.
2.
3.

Next, list three things you want to accomplish this month, your intermediate goals.
1.
2.
3.

Write a sentence telling about one of your long-range goals. It may only be a dream but if you want to pursue it, tell about it.

Answer these questions with yes or no.
1. Do your immediate goals connect in some way to your intermediate goals? ____

2. Will your intermediate goals help you reach your long-range one? ____
3. Are all of your goals realistic? ____

List three immediate and intermediate goals you can set now to help you reach your long-range one.

1.

2.

3.

Not only do people make unrealistic demands on themselves but they expect perfection from themselves. They see every failure as a defeat that they could have prevented.

Are you flexible enough not to condemn yourself for every failure, but rather to explore whether you fail for the right and not the wrong reasons? Some failures can be prevented and some can't. Are your failures justifiable?

As an example, I can recall two distinct incidents from my teaching days. I am not mathematically inclined. Oh, I'm sure if I set my mind to it and started with basic arithmetic, took the necessary courses and really applied myself I could learn mathematics, but presently I don't comprehend numerical concepts.

My first assignment as a student teacher was with a sixth-grade class. The lesson I was supposed to teach was division of mixed fractions, which I hadn't done since I was in grade school. I pored through the teacher's manual but it looked like Greek to me, so rather than try to prepare something that was impossible for me to understand, I decided I'd ad-lib the lesson and hope for the best.

The next morning I confidently announced that we were going to review division of mixed fractions. (Be honest. How many of you could do it?) I wrote an equation on the board and said, "Now, who can tell me what to do first?" Fortunately, there were kids who knew what to do and as I watched them do the problems step-by-step I caught on how to do them too.

No one knew I was unprepared, that I hadn't studied and that I hadn't carried out my responsibility. The lesson was a success; my supervising teacher even wrote a comment about how adeptly I had involved the students from the very start of the lesson. Yet, I had totally failed in the way I did that lesson, and it wasn't a *justifiable* failure because I could have prevented it.

Although the results were good, I failed because I went to class unprepared and had to bluff my way through the lesson. I was in no way responsible for the successful outcome.

A failure is a failure, whether it's visible or not. If you can do something to prevent or modify it and you don't, that failure isn't justifiable.

Another time I was going to teach a lesson to my second-grade class about using money. We were going to set up a store in the classroom and, using real money, learn how to buy, sell and make change. I taught several preparatory lessons and gave homework assignments asking parents to help their children count money and make change. I sent play money home for the children to practice with.

The day we had our store I discovered that about half of the class hadn't adequately done their homework. So instead of buying and selling we had to use the time reviewing initial concepts—counting by fives and tens and establishing the value of coins.

Superficially, the lesson was a failure. We hadn't

reached our goal and the results weren't what I'd intended but it was a justifiable failure. I had done all I could do and all of us learned a great deal. The children learned some arithmetic, but they also learned the value of being prepared, how to handle disappointment and the results of irresponsibility.

Record two things you've labeled as failures during the past few months, but instead of thinking of them in terms of results—I failed because it didn't turn out the way I'd planned it would or thought it should—decide whether they were justifiable or not.

Failure 1:
Expected result:

Actual outcome:

This was a justifiable/unjustifiable failure because:

Failure 2:
Expected result:

Actual outcome:

This was a justifiable/unjustifiable failure because:

Accept your justifiable failures as valuable learning experiences and determine how you can adjust your behavior to eliminate unreasonable ones. Remember, Christ has freed you to perform as best you can, not to be perfect. There are many times when you don't achieve the expected results. If you view those instances as failures then you'll start thinking of yourself as a failure and your self-image will be affected.

Are you flexible enough to think the best of yourself instead of the worst? Do you give yourself the benefit of a doubt? Self-condemnation is a sin and is very destructive because it is always accompanied by guilt. Romans 8:1 says, "There is therefore now no condemnation for those who are in Christ Jesus."

Since God, who has the right to condemn you, doesn't condemn you, you have no right to condemn yourself. So if you're condemning yourself for things that are past, all you can do is try not to make the same mistakes again, relax a little and say, "God has taken care of the past. He doesn't hold me guilty." Certainly, you're accountable for your actions but condemnation leads to guilt and guilt incapacitates you and affects your self-image.

Stop condemning yourself! Do your best and say, "I tried," instead of "I failed." Say, "My intentions were good," rather than, "It didn't turn out right." Say, "I'm sorry," instead of, "I'm guilty." Give yourself the benefit of a doubt!

Flexibilities

Is there anything you can do to make life a little easier and less intense, to decrease the unrealistic demands you make on yourself? What are some flexibilities that will help improve your self-image?

Develop a "you" trait, a trademark that's exclusively yours. A man I know always wears a bow tie; another one mystically combines two after-shave lotions to get a fragrance all his own. My college friend, Sally, always carried a dictionary with her and everybody knew her as "the girl with the dictionary." I have another friend who never goes anywhere without putting on something red, even if it's a hatpin on her scarf. People expect her to wear red. "You" traits are little individual touches that distinctly separate you from anyone else.

Allow for peculiarities. One of the most astonishing scientific facts in the universe is that *God never duplicates.* No snowflake, flower petal or insect wing is exactly like any other. Even identical twins have many distinguishing characteristics.

Since the creation of the world there has never been anyone exactly like you and there never will be. You are peculiar. The dictionary defines peculiar as distinctive, exclusive, unique, special, out of the ordinary. The Bible says that Jesus Christ "gave himself for us, that he might redeem us from all iniquity, and purify unto himself *a peculiar people*, zealous of good works" (Titus 2:14, *KJV*, italics added).

God expects and wants to preserve your peculiarities. Enjoy being different in the ways you are different. Be glad you're not like me, or your best friend, or your next-door neighbor.

From the time I was a child I was positive God had made a mistake when He gave me curly hair. I was raised during the Shirley Temple era, when all little girls had to wear curls like hers. Every morning before I could go to school I had to sit on a stool in the kitchen and my mom would carefully wrap a wet strand of hair around her finger, then meticulously scrape it off. The minute I would get out the door I'd shake my head, ruffle my hair with my fingers and do whatever I could to mess it up.

When I was in high school they didn't have all of the sophisticated hair products they have now, so I'd put waxed paper on strands of hair and iron on the wax to flatten the curl, but within half a day my hair would go t-w-a-a-n-g and spring back into curls. In college I entered the juice-can era. I'd plaster my hair with setting gel then roll it over orange juice cans or cardboard toilet paper centers. But, in the humid Kansas air, fluff rapidly turned to fuzz.

Finally, after I was married and started teaching school I began having my hair straightened. I thought, "Oh boy! Now, I'll finally have straight hair." But I quickly found that hair as curly as mine can't be completely straightened; also damaged hair wasn't worth the little bit of curl that did relax.

Then guess what happened! Naturals came into style and for the first time in my life I joyously let my hair do what it wants to do and the most amazing thing happened! I realized that God hadn't made a mistake and I've come to appreciate my peculiar curly hair. Differences are interesting. Why not enjoy yours?

Don't be an extremist. Extremists are rigid, dogmatic and unbending. They are inflexible. You want to be flexible enough to grow and change. If you're adamant about something, it's hard to backtrack to a less stringent position. Don't wall yourself in with unnecessary or narrow opinions and attitudes.

Image Preservers

How can flexibility help you in your relationships with others? Let's face it, you are affected by what you think others think of you and how they respond to you. Your self-image is intertwined in your interpersonal relationships. You want to be accepted and to contribute in positive ways. But there are certain flexible attitudes you have to assume in dealing with other people that keep you from feeling hurt, rejected or less than a whole person. What are these image preservers?

First reactions are usually surface reactions. Unfortunately, we all judge others on initial reactions and outward appearances. That's why you spent time this morning putting on makeup, carefully combing your hair, and thoughtfully deciding what to wear. You knew you were going to be looked at during the day, and we all know that first impressions count.

You aren't judged solely by your looks but also by how you present yourself. You may be an even-tempered, pleasant, humorous person but if someone meets you on an off-day when, for the first time in eight months, you're acting like the world's worst grouch, he or she will remember you as being grumpy.

You need to be flexible toward the initial reaction of others. Their opinions are often based on incomplete or inaccurate information, so are, to that extent, invalid. In 1 Samuel 16:7 God points out why it is wrong to dislike yourself because of what other people think of you. God was sending Samuel out to look for a king to replace Saul and He admonished him to "not look at his appearance or at the height of his stature . . . for God sees not as man sees, for man looks at the outward appearance, but the Lord looks at the heart."

In other words, the external superficials aren't what matter in a worthwhile relationship. If someone evaluates you based only on your background, education, or wardrobe it shouldn't adversely affect what you think of yourself.

How do you handle negative first reactions? When you meet someone for the first time and you sense they don't like you, do you feel: hurt, annoyed, worried, indifferent, frustrated, rejected, or that it's not your problem? List the words that best apply to you. Add others that describe your feelings.

What are two things you can do to counter your negative reactions?
1.
2.

People are not out to depersonalize you. If you're going to survive in the battle of everyday life you must be objective about statements or criticisms that are made to or about you. Not everyone who makes a negative remark or disagrees with you is attacking you as an individual. Sometimes they may be trying to help you. If you're subjective and are personally wounded by the many natural, normal conflicts that are an inevitable part of life, your self-image will suffer.

Generally, when you are criticized, do you feel: put down, rejected, angry, defensive, fearful, indifferent, grateful, hurt, annoyed, embarrassed? List any words that best apply to you. Add others that describe your feelings.

List two things that you can do that will make it easier for you to accept criticism.

1.

2.

Not everyone is going to like you. We all want to be liked so it hurts when, no matter what you do, someone rejects you. If someone dislikes you, you're responsible to evaluate why. If there are no obvious, valid reasons then there is nothing you can do. If they have a legitimate reason for disliking you, then perhaps you can remedy the situation. Maybe you can't. Our peculiarities and differences sometimes polarize us rather than pull us together. So as wonderful, sweet and great as you are, not everyone is going to like you.

When you are shunned and obviously disliked by someone who knows you, do you feel: infuriated, inadequate, wronged, judged, at fault, it's their loss, that you should try to make them like you or that you must find out why, indifferent? List all the words that best apply to you. Add others that describe your feelings.

Write the name of one person who doesn't like you. List as many reasons as you can why you think he or she doesn't like you. Put a check ($\checkmark$) by all of the valid reasons and an ex (X) by the invalid ones.
Name:
Reasons:

Not everyone is going to understand you. Sometimes you will be misunderstood. But you can't run around always trying to explain yourself to others, especially if they don't want to understand you. Don't feel you have to make excuses for everything you do, or you will reach a point when all you do is try to validate yourself.

Not everyone is going to understand what you're doing or why you're doing it. Not everyone will always trust your motives and accept your actions. You have to learn to say, "She didn't understand and there is nothing I can do about it."

Why do you think people sometimes misunderstand you? Check the appropriate blanks:

_____ I don't make myself clear.

_____ I don't communicate all the facts.

_____ I am timid.

_____ I anticipate they won't understand.

_____ They don't hear me out.

_____ I tend to be defensive.

_____ I don't disclose myself to others.

_____ Other (explain):

Not everyone is going to accept you. You can't be close to everybody you meet. Some people cross your path once; some are acquaintances. You enjoy being with them but there is no depth in the relationship.

Then there are people you care about and like to spend time with. You may see them frequently but you aren't emotionally close. The relationship is based on mutual activities and pleasurable experiences. Then you know a few people whom you call close friends. They're trustworthy confidants who accept you just as you are, the good with the bad, loving you because of, and in spite of, yourself.

There may be people you like and want to be close to who don't respond to you the same way. In some instances you won't be accepted or asked into an inner circle of friendship. If you're rejected, it doesn't mean there is something wrong with you. Don't let the normal course of human selectivity undermine your self-image.

Generally, when you are not accepted, do you feel: insecure, hurt, inadequate, angry, indifferent, that there's something wrong with you, or "that's life"? List the words that best apply to you. Add others that describe your feelings.

Write the name of a close friend and at least five reasons why you accept one another.
Name:
1.
2.
3.
4.
5.

Food for thought: the very reasons you accept each other could be the reasons why someone else would reject you.

Not everyone is going to agree with you. Wouldn't life be dull if everyone agreed about everything? Differences of opinion are inevitable because people are different. If you can accept disagreement as a normal by-product of our created uniqueness then you won't be threatened by it.

Disagreement doesn't imply dissatisfaction or dislike, it is simply a divergence of thought. When someone disagrees with you it doesn't mean one of you is right and the other is wrong. It means you have one opinion and someone else has another.

When someone openly and obviously disagrees with you, you may feel: threatened, angry, ridiculed, disappointed, helpless, disliked, defensive, misunderstood, indifferent, or that you can both have valid ideas. List the words that best apply to you. Add others that describe your feelings.

Write a simple, non-defensive response you can make when someone disagrees with you.

Not everyone is going to respond favorably to you. Some people are going to react negatively to you. Sometimes you'll be unfairly and harshly judged. You won't pass everyone's test as an A+ person. Since you can't please everybody, try to be the kind of person God wants you to be.

List four things about yourself that people, upon occasion, respond to unfavorably.

1.
2.
3.
4.

Are these abrasive personality traits or character defects? Do you dislike these things about yourself? If not, you should not let other people's judgment detract from your self-esteem.

Ultimate Emphasis

Accepting these seven image preservers as basic realities doesn't mean you should be insensitive to others or be callous toward them. Actually, your interpersonal relationships will improve as your objectivity increases and so will your self-image.

Ultimately, what matters isn't what others think of you but what you think of yourself. What counts are your motives, your methods and your maturity.

Your motives: Acts 24:16 says, "I also do my best to maintain always a blameless conscience both before God and before men." Whatever you do, do it with pure motives, based on valid, thoughtful reasons. If you do, even if others misunderstand, you'll be able to stand guiltless before them and God. Even if something you have done causes negative repercussions, God will take care of the results and uphold you if your motives are pure.

Your methods: Ephesians 5:1,2 says, "Be imitators of God, ... walk in love." Do you know what that means? It means you should treat others the way God would treat them. Imitate Him, and if they respond unfavorably, at least you know you used the best possible approach. If you aren't sure how God would act, I suggest you start reading through the Gospels. Read a portion daily and see how Jesus Christ acted.

One thing you'll discover is that love isn't permissive. There is a severity as well as a softness to Christ's love.

Love is filled with expectation; it's the most demanding thing in the world. Love never lets people go their own way; it sets boundaries. Sometimes love angers and temporarily alienates, but it always seeks to do what is best. Let love be your method.

Your maturity: Ephesians 4:14,15 says, "We are no longer to be children, tossed here and there by waves, and carried about by every wind of doctrine, by the trickery of men, by craftiness in deceitful scheming; but speaking the truth in love, we are to grow up in all aspects into Him, who is the head, even Christ." How do you handle the hassles of life? Do you let the opinions of men and their schemes control you? Are you like a little child, unsettled in what you believe, vacillating from one point of view to the other, running from the truth?

It's important that you mature. You are to *grow up*! Don't let unpleasant circumstances or other people keep you from being a whole, happy, well-adjusted person. No one can control your life unless you let him.

Be fundamentally flexible; accept yourself the way God accepts you, then go about the business of living and trust God with the results of your efforts.

REMEMBER: NOBODY'S PERFECT!

Workshop

As you read this chapter did you discover some inflexibilities in your life? This workshop can help you introduce some flexibilities that should improve your self-image.

1. Do you presently have a "you" trait, a trademark that's exclusively yours? ＿＿ yes ＿＿ no

2. If not, think of one (something that would be natural-
   ly you—not a contrived attention-getter) and write it
   here.

3. Are you truly appreciative of your God-created peculiarities? List as many of them as you can and write
   a positive about each one. For instance, if you're
   short you can date short or tall guys and wear very
   high heels without towering over anyone. Or, if you
   are a quiet person you can be a good listener and help
   others by lending an ear. Remember also, Jimmy
   Durante's lovable trademark is his big nose. He saw
   it as a positive!

   Peculiarity   *Positive*

4. Are you an extremist? List as many issues as you can
   where you draw a hard, unbending line and refuse to
   change or relent, even if it might be reasonable to do
   so.

7
IN HIS IMAGE

Are you starting to feel better about yourself? Hopefully, you're finding it easier to be more flexible and less intense about your faults and failures. As you've applied some of the principles and ideas from the previous chapters, have you been able to honestly and realistically change some negative behavior patterns, to love and accept yourself more fully?

The foundational steps you've taken so far should have been helpful in establishing self-esteem, but the key factor that is basic to positive self-development relates to your understanding of God and your attitudes and actions toward Him. *The single most important and decisive step you can take toward a permanent and healthy self-concept is to develop a God-oriented self-image.*

What is a God-oriented self-image? *God is truth*, so

to maintain a good self-image you must be truthful. If you lie or are a hypocrite your self-esteem suffers.

God is merciful, so to develop in a positive way you can't be defensive or vengeful.

God is just, so you must not be unfair or judgmental. Rather than catering to your ego you try to emulate God's divine nature.

Emulating God

You may wonder how you, an imperfect, finite, fallible, human being, can possibly imitate Almighty God. That's a reasonable concern. The answer is found in the creation story. "Then God said, 'Let us make man in *our image*, according to our likeness' " (Gen. 1:26, italics added). Did you know that we humans are the only part of God's creation that He made in His own image?

Grasp that fact—in God's image! God has an intellect and so do you. He has a will, emotions, a drive, a personality and a sense of humor and so do you. The lower animals don't laugh or cry; man alone is imitative of God in those ways.

Dr. J. Allan Peterson says, "Man is unique. God simply spoke and the whole universe came into being through His creative work. He did not speak man into existence but with special care He personally formed him and endowed him with many of His own divine characteristics. God did not create any superior or inferior people, there are only different people. Abilities and capabilities differ, each person has unique strengths which enable him to make a special contribution to God's plan. To refuse to accept yourself as God has made you is unconscious rebellion and is accusing Him of making a mistake."[1]

You were created in God's image, according to His likeness, therefore you can model His characteristics. Since God created you, He alone is ideally equipped to help you become all He created you to be. God wants you to be happy, fulfilled and productive. He holds you in high esteem so He can enable you to esteem yourself.

David realized how important we are to God. In Psalms 8:3-9, he sang about the Lord's glory and man's dignity: "When I consider Thy heavens, the work of Thy fingers, the moon and the stars, which Thou hast ordained; what is man, that Thou dost take thought of him? And the son of man, that Thou dost care for him? Yet Thou hast made him a little lower than God, and dost crown him with glory and majesty!"

What a concept! A perfect, holy, infinite God honors *you*! He has crowned you with glory and majesty. He wants you to model His ways.

If something is important to you, you are willing to invest time and effort in it. When a seamstress makes a dress she carefully chooses the right pattern. She wants one that is the proper size and style. With equal discretion she selects the fabric. It must be the right color and design. Then, as she sews, she painstakingly works with the raw materials so her finished product will turn out right.

You are important to God, He invested time and effort in your creation. Psalm 119:73 says, "Thy hands made me and *fashioned* me." As the Master Designer, He made a mental blueprint, carefully selected all the necessary human components, then meticulously molded them all together into the perfect end product He called "You." You are created exactly as God planned you to be.

Isaiah 64:8 uses the analogy of a potter and clay. "O Lord, Thou art our Father, we are the clay, and Thou our potter; and all of us are the work of Thy hand."

Last year when George, Brian and I went to the county fair I watched a young man make vases and bowls on his potter's wheel. He'd take a lump of dull, lifeless clay and meticulously work with it until it was structured exactly the way he'd imagined it should be. He would pause frequently and carefully study the size and shape of his creation, making sure it was balanced and curved in the right places.

I noticed an amazing thing about that clay. Not once during the entire process did it argue with the potter. It didn't say, "I'm gray and I wanted to be brown," or, "You're making me into a bud vase and I wanted to be a fruit bowl." It was totally pliable in the artist's hands; his to do with as he saw fit.

Many people have a poor self-image because they refuse to accept the way the Master Potter made them. They argue with God. They don't like what they are or how they look so they spend their lives complaining about what might have been instead of becoming the best of what God designed them to be. The apostle Paul exhorts those people: "Who are you, O man, who answers back to God? The thing molded will not say to the molder, 'Why did you make me like this,' will it? Or does not the potter have a right over the clay, to make from the same lump one vessel for honorable use, and another for common use?" (Rom. 9:20,21).

If you have been rebelling against who and what you are, you have been destroying your self-esteem and sense of worth. To develop a strong self-image you have to follow your God-created pattern. The ideal self-im-

109

age is realized as you conform to the image of God—as you understand and manifest His attributes.

Understanding God

Obviously, you cannot have a God-oriented self-image unless you first understand God. Many people, even Bible-reading, churchgoing Christians, don't actually know what God is like. It is imperative that you do because your image of yourself will never be any greater than your concept of God.

J.B. Phillips lists several misconceptions about God in his book *Your God Is Too Small.*[2] Some he names are Resident Policeman, Grand Old Man, Meek and Mild, the God of One Hundred Percent, Heavenly Bosom, God-in-a-Box and Managing Director.

In his book, *God's Will Is Not Lost,* John MacArthur notes that many people are afraid of God because they think "that God is a kind of 'cosmic killjoy,' stomping on everyone's fun and raining on parades."[3] The point is that if your concept of God is inaccurate or incomplete you will limit what God can do for and through you.

You need to know three things if you're going to elevate your sense of self-esteem: where did your concept of God originate; what is your concept of God, and what is God really like?

Where did your concept of God originate? Part of it stems from within you; ideas you have purposely or inadvertently conjured up so you can operate within the framework of what you want God to be rather than what He is actually like. You formed certain concepts so you can live as you wish and be comfortable about God, yet not be limited by Him.

110

Your thinking is also influenced by both the accurate as well as the erroneous written and spoken opinions of others. Your Sunday School, your parents, secular literature, the Bible and many other sources have contributed to your concept of God.

The most powerful influence is the one you were exposed to first, that of your own father. Everyone has had an earthly father, and whenever you listened to sermons or read the Bible the word "Father" was used in reference to God. So when you first thought about God, whether you were aware of it or not, you integrated your concept of Him with the image you had of your earthly father. Your concept of your human male parent is your basic concept of God.

J.B. Phillips observes that "the early conception of God is almost invariably founded upon the child's idea of his father. In adult years [many] are still obsessed with it, although it has actually nothing to do with their real relationship with the living God. It is nothing more than a parental hangover."[4]

I've observed some of these "parental hangovers" as I've taught and talked with people. One girl told me she couldn't place her trust in God because her own father was an "absentee" father who was gone a lot of time and who didn't like to be bothered when he was home. She said, "I always felt like I was infringing on God's time when I prayed so I just fended for myself as best I could, wanting a close relationship with the Lord but not knowing how to have one."

A lovely young lady of European descent shared that her father was an old-world patriarch so she pictured God as an unbending, insensitive dictator. She had to do things His way or else! She was afraid of God but she didn't love Him fully, neither did she experience His grace and compassion. One woman whose father had died when she was very young, admitted it was hard for her to understand God at all since she didn't know what a father was supposed to be like. Another girl said her father was very remote so she couldn't relate to God because she saw Him as standoffish and aloof.

My own father was likable, fun to be with and had a sense of humor. He was easygoing and approachable. He was there when I needed him and I could tell him what I thought without risking disapproval. Reflecting back, I can see that I have always related to God in the same way I did to my father.

This premise implies that if you had a good father-image you will have a proper concept of God. And conversely, if your father was a poor model you will have a limited or inappropriate concept of God.

If the latter is true, you no longer have to let it negatively affect your evaluation of God. Simply start looking at God in *contrast* to your father rather than in comparison to him. Instead of thinking God is cruel and unfair because your father was, *contrast* God's kindness and justice with your earthly father's imperfections. As you draw these distinctions you will break down spiritual barriers that have existed for many years. You will broaden your concept of God.

What is your concept of God? I once heard a story about a little boy who was busily drawing a picture. As his father passed, he paused and asked, "What are you drawing, Johnny?"

"A picture of God," Johnny answered.

"But you can't do that," the father insisted. "No one knows what God looks like."

Undaunted, the child replied, "Well, when I finish they will."

What would you draw in your picture if you were Johnny? Could you pen a true portrait of God? In the space provided write five things you believe are true about God.

Now check your list against these six common misconceptions about God.

• Misconception 1: God is indulgent. Some people believe that, because God wants you to be happy, He will let you do anything you want without penalizing you. They think of Him as an indulgent, pampering parent. This misconception relates to a misunderstanding of God's love.

We've already seen that *agape* love is the most demanding force in the world. God expects your obedience in return for His love. Jesus said, "If you love Me, you will keep My commandments. . . . He who has My commandments and keeps them, he it is who loves Me" (John 14:15,21). God doesn't want you to obey so He can hedge you in, but so He can direct your life in a positive way.

God also disciplines in love. He does this in two ways. He may let you reap what you sow or He may intervene with direct punishment.

"The righteousness of the blameless will smooth his

way, but the wicked will fall by his own wickedness" (Prov. 11:5). God doesn't have to strike you with lightning to punish you; He knows you'll be trapped by your own devices, that you will reap what you sow. But He could choose to discipline you directly: "For when he punishes you, it proves that he loves you. When he whips you it proves you are really his child. . . . God's correction is always right and for our best good, that we may share his holiness" (Heb. 12:6,10, *TLB*).

• Misconception 2: You can hide from God. You can't because God is *omnipresent*—He is everywhere. This misconception is the product of your effort to conceal your sin. You don't ever want to hide from God when you are doing what you think would please Him, but only when you're doing that which is contrary to what He expects of you. You rationalize and say, "No one will know." But God always does.

Psalms 139:7-12 says: "I can never get away from my God! If I go up to heaven, you are there; if I go down to the place of the dead, you are there. If I ride the morning winds to the farthest oceans, even there your hand will guide me, your strength will support me. If I try to hide in the darkness, the night becomes light around me. For even darkness cannot hide from God" *(TLB)*. You can refuse to face the reality of God but you can never hide from Him.

• Misconception 3: You can bribe God. Some people try to make bargains with God: If you do this, God, I'll do that. This is foolish because God is *sovereign*. He is a self-determining personality and no one can tell Him what to do or how to do it.

You can't bribe God because He is just and it would be unfair of Him to cater to your wants and wishes for human reasons. He must act according to His divine will and nature.

This doesn't mean that God is uncaring or unresponsive but rather that He is ultra-sensitive to your human frailty. He wants you to ask for things, rather than bargain for them, so He can protectively withhold the harmful for the good, the least for the most. "And we are sure of this, that he will listen to us whenever we ask him for anything in line with his will. And if we really know he is listening when we talk to him and make our requests, then we can be sure that he will answer us" (1 John 5:14,15, *TLB*).

Another reason you can't bribe God is because He is *faithful.* He'll never do what isn't best for you, no matter how much you want it. Usually your bribes fall far short of God's desires for you. He is "able to do exceeding abundantly beyond *all that we ask or think*" (Eph. 3:20, italics added).

• Misconception 4: You can fool God. You can fool other people, and sometimes yourself, but we've already seen that God doesn't have to listen to your words or watch your actions in order to understand you; He reads your heart. You are deluding yourself if you think you can fool God.

God is *omniscient.* He has perfect knowledge of the past, present and future. He knows what you're going to do or say before you make a move or say a word: "Thou dost know when I sit down and when I rise up; . . . even before there is a word on my tongue, behold, O Lord, Thou dost know it all." He discerns your motives: "Thou dost understand my thought from afar" (Ps. 139: 2,4).

• Misconception 5: God will tolerate evil. Have you

noticed how our society has developed degrees of right and wrong? It's bad to tell a big black lie but acceptable to tell a little white one. You can cheat on an exam or your income tax or pad your expense account and it's not wrong unless you get caught, but you must not rob the neighborhood liquor store.

To God, sin is sin. Because He is *holy*—pure, separate and set apart from *all* degrees of evil—He cannot tolerate sin in any form. The lie you tell about your next-door neighbor is as abhorrent to Him as murder; He doesn't gradate sin. Habakkuk 1:13 clearly states, "Thine [God's] eyes are too pure to approve evil, and Thou canst not look on wickedness with favor." God cannot tolerate any form of evil.

• Misconception 6: God condemns man. God, the great Judge, has acquitted those of us who have accepted Christ. He is *gracious* and *merciful.* Romans 8:33,34 says: "Who would dare to accuse us, whom God has chosen? The judge himself has declared us free from sin. Who is in a position to condemn? Only Christ, and Christ died for us, Christ rose for us, Christ reigns in power for us, Christ prays for us!" *(Phillips).*

Since God doesn't condemn you, how are you condemned? Why are you condemned? Your sin condemns you and severs your relationship with God. God is holy in character and He cannot tolerate sin. Isaiah says God has hidden His face from the sinner (see Isa. 59:2). Who is a sinner? "All have sinned and fall short of the glory of God" (Rom. 3:23). Therefore sin is what condemns you. But because God loves you, He wants to restore your relationship with Him so He provided a way to reestablish communication and erase the condemnation: "Christ died for the ungodly.... God demonstrates His own love toward us, in that while we were yet sinners, Christ died for us" (Rom. 5:6,8).

God provides the only way out of the condemnation you brought on yourself by sinning. If you accept God's restorative gift of love you aren't condemned. "For God so loved the world, that He gave His only begotten Son, that whoever believes in Him should not perish, but have eternal life. For God did not send the Son into the world to judge the world; but that the world should be saved through Him" (John 3:16,17). "There is therefore now no condemnation for those who are in Christ Jesus" (Rom. 8:1).

If you are nurturing these or any other misconceptions about God, you are hindering your personal development. You can't establish a God-oriented self-image if you are underestimating God's love, trying to hide from Him, cheating yourself by denying His lordship or refusing His release from your condemnation.

How can you correct your misconceptions and find out what God is really like? You go to the Bible, God's Word. It is filled with verbal portraits of His attributes and characteristics.

Psalm 102:24 begins, "I say, 'O my God, do not take me away in the midst of my days.' " This brief sentence contains two important concepts. First, God is a *personal* God, not some puppeteer who randomly pulls the strings of your life. The psalmist cried, "O *my* God." He has a personal relationship with his Lord. Second, God is powerful enough to control life and death; He is *omnipotent.*

The psalmist continued: "Thy years are throughout all generations." God is not limited by time or space. He is everywhere at all times. He is *omnipresent.*

In verse 25 you get a glimpse of His *creativity, beauty, power* and *sovereignty:* "Of old Thou didst found the earth; and the heavens are the work of Thy hands." Think of the vastness of the universe, the beauty of the heavens and the earth, the intricate process that takes place as a seed germinates and pushes through the soil toward the sun. God thought all of it up, determined what to do, then He created it. Immense power, intellect and creativity were required to make a vast solar system and delicate, perfumed roses. God didn't create only balance and order in the universe but color, sound and touch. Surely a God who created pleasures such as laughter and music is sensitive to you, the ultimate product of His handiwork.

Verse 26 further reveals the character of God: "Even they [the heavens] will perish, but Thou dost endure." God is *eternal.* He has always existed and He always will. He is set apart from time so He can nullify your past and secure your future.

As the verse continues you discover yet another attribute: God is *immutable.* "All of them [the heavens] will wear out like a garment; like clothing Thou wilt change them, and they will be changed. But Thou art the same." God never changes. If He could He wouldn't be dependable and who would want a God who can't be trusted?

The passage ends with another statement about His eternality: "Thy years will not come to an end." If there are that many concepts about God in one small passage, imagine how many the entire Bible contains!

Yet, in love, God went a step beyond His written Word and sent us the living Word: Jesus Christ. God knows it is difficult for us to understand Him. He is a

118

Spirit and we cannot relate to Him through our senses as we do to our physical universe. So He sent His Son as a visible explanation of His divine nature, to make it easier for us to get to know Him.

As a teacher, I understand the immense value of audiovisual aids. They are concrete learning tools. When I taught second grade, every year we raised silkworms. We watched the entire life cycle, from the time I put the tiny dot of a black egg into a box until the thread was spun. No film, no still pictures, no story could have portrayed the process as vividly as did the actual experience. The children felt the eggs, watched them hatch, heard the worms actually crunch their feast of mulberry leaves and saw them spin delicate strands of thread into cocoons.

In a way, Jesus Christ is God's visual aid to us. John 1:14,18 explains that, "The Word became flesh, and dwelt among us, and we beheld His glory, glory as of the only begotten from the Father, full of grace and truth.... No man has seen God at any time; the only begotten God, who is in the bosom of the Father, *He has explained Him*." If you want to know what God is like, look at Christ. Colossians 1:15 says "He is the image of the invisible God." The author of the epistle to the Hebrews says that Christ is the radiance of God's nature (see Heb. 1:3).

To develop a God-oriented self-image, pattern yourself after Jesus Christ. Study the Gospels and find out how He acted and reacted when He was trapped in human circumstances similar to the ones you face every day. How did He handle anger, injustice and fear? When did He back off and when did He pursue? He is your model.

Paul tells the Romans that God has destined every person who has a relationship with Christ "to be molded into the image of His Son [and share inwardly His likeness]" (Rom. 8:29, *AMP*). Therein lies the secret of a God-oriented self-image that has quality and is adequate: God molding you into the image of His Son—the only perfect person who ever lived. But this conformity doesn't just happen. It evolves as you get to know yourself and God deeply and intimately, as you walk with Him in a faith-love relationship.

What are some things you can expect from a God-oriented self-image? Sharper creativity, inner beauty, graciousness, humility, truthfulness, compassion, a forgiving nature and a strength you have never experienced before, because they stem from the ultimate power source—God Himself. You will be free to develop your potential to be yourself in the fullest sense because if "the Son shall make you free, you shall be free indeed" (John 8:36).

REMEMBER: THE SINGLE, MOST IMPORTANT AND DECISIVE STEP YOU CAN TAKE TOWARD A PERMANENT AND HEALTHY SELF-CONCEPT IS TO DEVELOP A GOD-ORIENTED SELF-IMAGE.

Workshop

Look up each Scripture reference and complete the sentence to explain how God can help improve your self-image in each area that is listed.

Jude 24   *Failure*

God will prevent unnecessary failures in my life by:

1 Peter 5:7   *Worry*
Instead of worrying I should:

1 John 4:16-18   *Fear*
God can remove fear from my life through the presence of:

Matthew 10:28-31   *Security*
God cares for me so deeply that He:

1 Corinthians 15:58   *Productivity*
I can be certain everything I do will count for something if:

Hebrews 11:1,6   *Faith*
Faith in God will result in a more positive self-image because:

1 Corinthians 14:33   *Confusion*
God can replace the confusion in my life with _____, because:

1 Timothy 6:10,11   *Goals*

God will help me set my sights on such positive achievements as:

2 Timothy 1:7   *Strength*

I do not have to succumb to my human weaknesses because God has given me:

Notes

1. J. Allan Peterson with Elven and Joyce Smith, *Two Become One* (Wheaton: Tyndale House, 1973), p. 31.
2. J.B. Phillips, *Your God Is Too Small* (New York: The Macmillan Co., 1961). p. 5.
3. John MacArthur, Jr., *God's Will Is Not Lost* (Wheaton: Victor Books, 1973), p. 4.
4. J.B. Phillips, *Your God Is Too Small* (New York: The Macmillan Co., 1961), p. 19.

HOW TO 8
COPE WITH THE
HUMAN CONDITION

To err is human, an old adage observes. So is being selfish, being greedy, laughing, crying, failing, and mistrusting your fellowman. Any way you view it, your humanity is a limiting factor.

Heroes such as Superman and Tarzan have universal appeal because they transcend the human condition, unlimited by their physical structure or current circumstances. Yet, in everyday life even the most "superhuman" people are precariously weak.

I was reminded of this as I was watching a pro-football game on television the other day. One of the key players, a hulking, well-trained, perfectly-honed specimen, landed in the wrong position when he was tackled and his shoulder instantly snapped out of joint. When the game was over, a camera panned the bench where the losing team was sitting. There, over 30 super-heroes sat crying, their heads hung sorrowfully, distraught at their loss. Their emotional frailty was obvious. We all fall prey to our human condition.

At this point, you may be wondering if you can ever overcome all the obstacles that are negatively affecting your self-image. You are frail, weak, and fragile. You are physiologically and emotionally vulnerable. But you are not hopeless!

In this chapter you're going to study the success story of a man who had a good self-image. He probably had more deficiencies and past mistakes to overcome than you do. He cheated, lied, betrayed his position, committed adultery, misused his authority and was a murderer, but he had a good self-image. That man was David, whose dramatic life story spans three books of the Bible. He rose from being a humble shepherd boy to become king of Israel, a direct predecessor of the Messiah. And despite his sin and disgraceful misconduct he maintained a perspective and equilibrium about himself that can serve as an example to all of us who feel trapped by our human frailty but want to conquer it.

Romans 15:4 says, "For whatever was written in earlier times was written for our instruction, that through perseverance and the encouragement of the Scriptures we might have hope." Few of you will ever make more or worse mistakes than David did. If he survived victorious, so can you if you study and follow his example.

David looked at himself realistically; he saw the good and the bad, his obedience and his disobedience, his service and his sin but he never lost sight of the positive, even when his performance was all negative.

Why did David survive when others might have given up and caved in? David succeeded for one reason: he knew God. He trusted his Lord and relied on what God could do in his life to help him, improve him and change him. He had the faith to take God at His word.

Even after his hands had shed innocent blood he never once thought God would take away his salvation. His lament wasn't, "Please don't keep me out of heaven for what I've done." Rather, in Psalm 51:12, he cried to the Lord to "Restore *the joy* of my salvation." He understood that he hadn't lost his eternal position, merely the benefits of it. Keep in mind that you have the same freedom in your relationship with God that David had, if you've trusted the Lord with your salvation.

Let's dig into Scripture and see how David handled life situations that tend to detract from self-image, ones that you also face and must overcome.

How David Coped with Depression

Recent statistics show that depression is the most common emotional illness in the United States today. There are many diverse causes of depression; some are physical but the vast majority are psychological. They are difficult to isolate and define. But when depression strikes, it diminishes your sense of self-worth and accomplishment.

We can see this in David's words. When David penned Psalm 13 he was caving in under his circumstances. His predecessor, King Saul, had persecuted him for a prolonged period of time and he had reached the point where he simply couldn't take the pressure. He felt so isolated and alienated that he accused God of forgetting him. In anguish, he moaned, "How long, O Lord? Wilt Thou forget me forever? How long wilt Thou hide Thy face from me? How long shall I take counsel in my soul, having sorrow in my heart all the day? How long will my enemy be exalted over me?" (Ps. 13:1,2).

David was separated from God. Communication had been broken. His human efforts had failed and he thought God had deserted him. David had let his circumstances alienate him from God.

The major cause of his depression was that he had no sense of God's presence. God was still there but David wasn't relating to Him.

The same thing can happen to you when you are overcome by your circumstances. Rather than remembering there is a loving, sovereign God who cares about and controls your life, you relate only to yourself and your problem and end up "having sorrow in your heart all the day." The blessing and security of God's presence in your life are gone and you sink into the depths of despair.

But must you stay there? What did David do next?

He refused to accept the situation as it was. He expected God to respond to him. He cared enough about himself to take a step toward the Lord and away from his self-pity. My guess is that his next words weren't a soft-spoken, remorseful request but rather, with clenched fist, he screamed to God, "Consider and answer me, O Lord, my God." (Notice he said *my* God. Already the personal relationship was being restored.) "Enlighten my eyes, lest I sleep the sleep of death" (Ps. 13:3).

David, the spiritual giant whom God Himself called "a man after My own heart" (see 1 Sam. 13:14), was so depressed that he didn't care whether he lived or died. He honestly, openly told God, "You'd better cheer me up because if you don't I may die." He wasn't ashamed to admit that the depression existed or to ask for help in overcoming it. And see what happened when he did!

He started focusing onto the character of God. He started looking at past positives, how he had trusted God before and the Lord had been tenderly merciful. David didn't believe God had actually forgotten him but he *felt* as if He had because he was relying on himself rather than on God's grace. So he exchanged his mournful cry of "Wilt Thou forget me forever?" to words of joy and praise: "My heart [that just moments ago was full of sorrow] shall *rejoice* in Thy salvation. I will sing to the Lord, because He has dealt bountifully with me" (Ps. 13:5,6).

As David concentrated on God he experienced a mental revival. His depression dissolved. God hadn't changed, but his approach had.

If this procedure worked for David it will work for you, maybe not as rapidly nor as easily, but it *will* work. If your depression is a prolonged one, you may need professional guidance. But when everyday circumstances get you down and you lose your emotional perspective and equilibrium, is there some way you can cope with the depression? You might try the following method:

1. Admit you are depressed. Don't try to keep a quivering, stiff upper lip.
2. Verbalize your feelings, no matter how dire or foolish they may seem. In the space below write words or phrases to describe how you feel when you are depressed. Say them aloud several times.

127

3. Focus on God, not on yourself. Reading Scripture is a good way to do this. Especially uplifting are Psalms 103 through 150. Read one several times if necessary. List all the positives it tells about God. List all of the responses it indicates you should have toward Him.

Positives about God   *Responses toward God*

4. Now, list all of the human positives that are presently stacked in your favor.

5. Praise God for them and think about His bountiful dealings with you. Repeat them aloud, "God I praise you that ..."

6. Expect a positive response from the Lord and yourself.

How David Coped with Life Performance

In the first verse of Psalm 15 David asks the question we all must ask if we are going to be happy. Basically we need to know, "How shall I live so as to satisfy myself, my fellow man and my God?" David knew the answer to that question. He had a basic philosophy. He didn't always stick to it but he was aware that certain standards and values are required if you want to live a successful, fruitful life. He recited his code of life in this psalm.

David's philosophy was quite simple: a person can perform well, be happy and abide with God if he "walks with integrity, and works righteousness, and speaks truth in his heart. He does not slander with his tongue, nor does evil to his neighbor, nor takes up a reproach against his friend; in whose eyes a reprobate is despised, but who honors those who fear the Lord; he swears to his own hurt, and does not change; he does not put out his money at interest, nor does he take a bribe against the innocent" (Ps. 15:1-5). If these are your ethics, David concluded, you "will never be shaken."

Do you, as David did, have a basic philosophy about the way you should live your life? Do you understand what is required of you, what will make you happy and why you believe the things you believe? Such knowledge is the essential basis for a good self-image.

How do your life-performance ethics compare with David's God-inspired ones? Put an ex (X) by each one you believe is part of your basic philosophy. Circle the ex if you actively practice that philosophy as part of your life-style.

_____ I have principles and act according to them rather than catering to circumstances or certain individuals or groups.

_____ I try to serve others in practical ways.

_____ I am truthful with myself.

_____ I am truthful with others.

_____ I speak well of others or keep silent.

_____ I am not negatively critical or judgmental of my friends but enjoy them for what they are.

_____ I associate with people who have what I consider to be good morals and a godly life-style.

_____ I accept responsibility for my failures and faults rather than blaming others or circumstances.

_____ I am honest and fair in my dealings with others.

_____ I honor the Lord in my life.

How David Coped with Frustration

Life is full of frustration. Plans go wrong and things don't turn out the way you'd hoped or expected. You waste time and energy, make foolish decisions and sometimes can't seem to accomplish a thing, no matter how hard you try. Eventually, you lose your perspective.

How did David cope with similar frustrations and keep his peace and perspective? He maintained a quiet confidence and inner security by meditating upon God and His Word. In Psalm 23 we see how David reflected on and pondered the sufficiency of God. David readily acknowledged that "He makes me lie down in green pastures; He leads me beside quiet waters, He restores my soul; He guides me in the paths of righteousness" (Ps. 23:2,3).

He compared his helplessness with the strength of a sovereign God, the sorrows of the past with the joy he could experience in the present, his inconsequential desires with the satisfaction of knowing God and the impermanence of his humanity with the certainty of eternity, boldly declaring, "I will dwell in the house of the Lord forever" (Ps. 23:6).

David pictured himself being led by God, provided for by God, protected by God, pampered by God and coexisting with God. Anytime you start feeling worthless, think of yourself in that way. Concentrate on God's abundant, gracious provisions. *You shall not want.* You have God, so lack nothing; you have the strength to live life and your needs are being met. *He makes you to lie down in green pastures ... leads you beside quiet waters ... restores your soul.* You don't have to be frustrated, God's peace is available if you'll take it.

David knew his Lord would uphold and comfort him during the most fearful and awesome of human experiences: "Even though I walk through the valley of the shadow of death ... Thou art with me" (Ps. 23:4). God is with you, to support you during your trials and to calm your spirit. All you must do is follow Him. His route is the peaceful path of righteousness.

How David Coped with Fear

Recently, the newspaper carried the tragic story of a family who burned to death. Their house caught fire and, because their home had wrought iron bars on the windows and triple-locked doors, they could not get out. Ironically, the devices they installed to keep out intruders and protect themselves, caused their deaths. In a manner of speaking, their fear killed them.

Every minute of every day danger lurks in the nooks and crannies of your existence. There are physical dangers. You never know what is going to happen next. Life doesn't come with a guarantee. There are emotional pitfalls.

If you are having an internal struggle you may be fearful, afraid to do something, say something or attack the problem. How can you, instead of shrinking in fear and anxiety, face each day with a courage and conviction that will enhance your self-respect?

Once again, David believed that God is the answer. He relied on the fact that "the Lord is my light and my salvation; whom shall I fear? The Lord is the defense of my life; whom shall I dread?" (Ps. 27:1).

One of the most beloved stories in the Bible is that of the gutsy, courageous, young shepherd boy who, on sheer faith alone, fought and defeated the giant Philistine enemy, Goliath. Instead of being afraid, David was indignant: "Who is this uncircumcised Philistine, that he should taunt the armies of the living God?" (1 Sam. 17:26). Rather than surrender to his fears he activated his faith. "The Lord who delivered me from the paw of the lion and from the paw of the bear, He will deliver me from the hand of this Philistine" (1 Sam. 17:37).

David had a twofold perspective about fear and how to counter it.

First, he believed that if you have fears you should seek God and He will deliver you from them. He knew you cannot lock them out, run from them or deny them. David said, "I sought the Lord and He delivered me from my fears." David's formula for conquering fear was to disclose his fears to God and discuss them with Him. When you do likewise, He will answer you and deliver you from them in much the same way a mother allays the fears of her child. God draws you close to Him and loves you so deeply that your fears disappear. First John 4:18 says, "Perfect love casts out fear." When God's perfect love is operating in your life your fears dissolve into a sense of warmth and well-being.

Second, David's perspective was that you should compare your fears to God's power. God is your light so there is no need to fear any real or imagined darkness. God is your salvation. He can save you. Why should you be afraid? God is the defense of your life. With Him upholding you, what do you have to dread? David knew that faith in a supernatural God extinguishes mortal fear. Once you have surrendered your fears to God and replaced them with faith you can get on about the business of living with a calmness and certainty that will allow you to think more highly of yourself.

How David Coped with Guilt

Whatever you have to feel guilty about cannot be any greater than David's sin. Second Samuel 11 recounts David's sin. He lusted after and committed adultery with Bathsheba, whose husband, Uriah the Hittite, was a soldier. When David found out she was pregnant, he tried to trick Uriah into leaving his assigned duties and sleeping with his wife so she and the king could pawn off their illegitimate child as Uriah's heir.

Uriah was too honorable to desert his post. So David further misused his position as king and commander of the army by trying to get Uriah so drunk that he would forget his military obligations, go AWOL, and have sexual relations with his wife.

When that didn't work, in desperation, David plotted to kill Bathsheba's husband by sending him into battle. His instructions to the general of his army were to "place Uriah in the front line of the fiercest battle and withdraw from him, so that he may be struck down and die." That was premeditated, cold-blooded murder. Not only did Uriah die but several innocent servants perished as well.

So Bathsheba was finally free to marry David. Verse 27 of 2 Samuel 11 says, "The thing that David had done was evil in the sight of the Lord."

David couldn't escape the consequences of his acts. God severely disciplined this man He so dearly loved;

133

but the chastisement of the Lord was bearable. David accepted that. It was his guilt that weighed him down, preyed on his mind and affected his body and soul.

Guilt is a debilitating emotion and is doubly devastating when it is grounded in sin. When you violate God's standards and your conscience, you suffer recrimination until you make restitution.

David's guilt festered within him until it was intolerable. He was king of Israel, one of God's anointed. He knew the law and he knew the Lord. He stood without excuse before a holy God, his guilt burning like a gnawing cancer in his soul. Finally, when he could bear it no longer, David spewed forth all of his buried remorse. "Against Thee, Thee only, I have sinned, and done what is evil in Thy sight" (Ps. 51:4). How did David cope progressively with his culpability?

Like many of us David tried to hide from it and deny the reality of it. When he could no longer do that, he once again relied on the character of God and pleaded for mercy: "Be gracious to me, O God, according to Thy lovingkindness; according to the greatness of Thy compassion blot out my transgressions" (Ps. 51:1).

What a simple supplication after such dastardly deeds. Yet, after all he'd done, David had the courage to ask God not to judge him too harshly. He was guilty and wanted forgiveness. He felt tainted and dirty and wanted cleansing. "Wash me . . . cleanse me . . . purify me," he entreated.

Next, David tried to bury his guilt. But that didn't work either. He found that to bury his guilt was self-destructive. David lamented the physical and spiritual results of his buried sin and guilt. "When I kept silent about my sin, my body wasted away through my groaning all day long . For day and night Thy hand was heavy upon me; my vitality was drained away as with fever-heat of summer" (Ps. 32:3,4).

It is easy to see how guilt can obliterate your self-image; it renders both body and spirit impotent and ineffective. Guilt must be released!

Finally, David confessed both his sin and guilt. "I know my transgressions, and my sin is ever before me" (Ps. 51:3). Bottled up sin causes guilt. Guilt, an ever-present reality, keeps you from performing and functioning wholly and fully in the Lord's will. When you are out of God's will your life is at best one big blunder. Eventually, you conclude that you are worthless. Your self-image wanes.

Sin and guilt are spiritual abscesses which, if left untreated, infect your entire life. You, like David, must acknowledge your transgressions because you can't eliminate or change them until you do.

After David admitted and relinquished his sin and guilt, he then relied on the creative power of a gracious and forgiving God to help him reestablish his self-image. "Create in me a clean heart, O God, and renew a steadfast spirit within me" (Ps. 51:10). Along with a clean heart and a desire to start doing what was right, he asked for one other thing—joy. His specific request was, "Make me to hear joy and gladness. . . . Restore to me the joy of Thy salvation" (Ps. 51:8,12).

Guilt cancels joy. David had been miserably unhappy. He boldly asked God for activated joy, knowing that once his sin and guilt were gone he could experience an abundant life. The same is true for you.

If you are suffering from guilt, why not try doing what David did?

1. Acknowledge your transgression(s). Pick one thing you feel most guilty about and write it in the space below.

2. Verbally confess it to God. In his confession, David asked God to be gracious and merciful to him and to blot out his sin.

3. Ask for cleansing and joy. Since cleansing involves removing dirt, write three reasons why you should not feel guilty anymore.
   a.
   b.
   c.

4. Ask God to give you a steadfast spirit. Write one thing you can do to keep from repeating the act you were feeling guilty about.

5. Sometimes part of acknowledging your sin is to go to a person you have hurt or wronged and ask forgiveness. If the incident you are guilty about needs to be resolved with another person, write how you can make restitution.

David knew he wasn't perfect, that he needed God's help to develop a good self-image; he knew he couldn't do it on his own. Neither can you, no matter how hard you try or how badly you want to. You need God's assistance for several reasons. You are too familiar with yourself to see yourself in perspective. You tend to candy-coat, ignore or rationalize what you do and too readily condemn or excuse yourself.

You aren't able to see yourself the way God sees you. The darkness of sin blinds you to the truth. Your knowledge of yourself will always be imperfect so it must be filtered through God's perfect vision. God alone can show you yourself as you really are.

How David Coped with Doubt

How did David cope with the uncertainty of self? He asked God to reveal several things to him.

First, he asked God to unmask his heart. "Search me, O God, and know my heart" (Ps. 139:23). He wanted to understand rather than be deceived by it.

Next, David said, "Try me and know my anxious thoughts" (Ps. 139:23). In other words, he wanted God to test his doubts and opinions and show him which of his beliefs were right and which were incorrect. If you truly want to improve your self-image, you must ask God to do the same for you. If you have false illusions and wrong opinions about yourself, God will divulge them to you if you sincerely want to know. You may find that there are some things you dislike that God values greatly and you may cherish some opinions that God doesn't like at all.

Finally, David asked God to see if there were any hurtful ways in him; if he was causing any pain, grief or unhappiness for himself, his God or others. David was uncertain about himself so he was willing to be tried, to lay his life open to God's searchlight so that He could expose and eliminate the dirt in his heart, his doubts and erroneous ideas and harmful behavior patterns.

The strongest testimony corroborating the strength of

137

David's self-image is found in 2 Samuel 12. David had been avoiding the issue of his sin and guilt so the Lord sent the prophet, Nathan, to convict him of his transgression. When the king finally confessed and repented, Nathan assured him that "the Lord has taken away your sin; you shall not die" (2 Sam. 12:13). But he also predicted that David would suffer dire consequences for his villainy. The prophet foretold, "The child also that is born to you shall surely die" (2 Sam. 12:14).

I can only imagine what thoughts permeated David's consciousness at that moment. All the plots and contrivances, the attempted cover-up and the wasted lives had been for nothing. The child he and Bathsheba had conceived in adultery would die. His sin would cost him his child's life.

Exactly as Nathan prophesied, the child became gravely ill. The Bible tells us that David "inquired of God for the child," then he fasted and went and laid on the ground all night. Some members of his household encouraged him to get up and to eat, but he refused. I am convinced that during this time David was in deep prayer, pleading for further mercy, reliving his mistakes, recounting them to God and mourning in advance the death of his son. In Psalm 51 he lamented, "My sin is ever before me." I think David wanted to remember what he'd done. He wanted to face the emotional, physical and spiritual consequences because true repentance means that although you forsake your sin, you don't forget it; you remember so you don't do it again.

Seven days later his son died. David had been acting so strangely that the servants were afraid to tell him the child was dead. They said, "Behold, while the child was still alive, we spoke to him and he did not listen to our voice. How then can we tell him that the child is dead, since he might do himself harm?" (2 Sam. 12:18).

Obviously, they didn't understand David's actions. They thought he was so overcome with grief and guilt that he might commit suicide. They were quite surprised at David's reaction when he heard of his son's death. He got up, washed, anointed himself, changed his clothes, went into the house of the Lord to worship, then went back to his house to eat.

The servants couldn't believe it. They said, "What is this thing you have done? While the child was alive, you fasted and wept; but when the child died, you arose and ate food" (2 Sam. 12:21).

David's response was staggering, "While the child was still alive, I fasted and wept; for I said, 'Who knows, the Lord may be gracious to me, that the child may live. But now he has died; why should I fast? Can I bring him back again? I shall go to him, but he will not return to me" (2 Sam. 12:22,23).

David accepted the responsibility for what he had done. But rather than wallow in guilt and self-pity, he did all he could to rectify the situation and willingly accepted God's chastisement. Although the Lord didn't spare the child, He blessed David with the hope that someday he would be reunited with his son. God also blessed David and Bathsheba with another male heir, Solomon.

There was only one reason why David could endure such guilt, such discipline, such pain and not lose his sense of self-worth. He knew God deeply and intimately. "David saw God in everything. We lose sight of the cause in the instrument and are not so devout as he. We see law where he saw a Person."[1]

In Psalm 103 David lists some things he knew about God that helped him sustain his self-esteem.

1. He knew that whatever God allowed or caused to happen to him would be beneficial. "Bless the Lord, O my soul, and forget none of His benefits" (v. 2). He knew that even the painful lessons he learned through God's discipline were helpful, productive experiences.

2. He knew that God is a forgiving God. He "pardons *all* your iniquities" (v. 3). David knew that God wanted to remove his guilt as badly as he wanted it removed.

3. He knew God could save him. He "redeems your life from the pit" (v. 4). David trusted God to restore him and keep him from eternal damnation.

4. He knew that God would rather give him what would help him than give him what he deserved. He "crowns you with lovingkindness and compassion" (v. 4). David knew he deserved to die. He had committed capital crimes yet God chose to spare him.

5. He knew that God is patient. "The Lord is . . . slow to anger" (v. 8). David knew that God acts in accord with His character rather than in response to our sin.

6. He knew that God doesn't hold grudges. "He will not always strive with us; nor will He keep His anger forever" (v. 9). David knew that no matter what he had done, God would eventually prepare a way to resolve it.

7. He knew that God wanted to love him more than He wanted vengeance against him. "He has not dealt with us according to our sins, nor rewarded us according to our iniquities" (v. 10). David knew that, although he had readily and easily betrayed the Lord, God would not retaliate by betraying or forsaking him.

8. He knew that God doesn't merely forgive; He also forgets. "As far as the east is from the west, so far has

He removed our transgressions from us" (v. 12). David knew that God could literally erase the past and give him a fresh start.

9. He knew that God understands our human condition. "He Himself knows our frame; He is mindful that we are but dust" (v. 14). David knew that God empathized with his faults, failings and weaknesses; that He completely understood his human imperfection and limitations.

God hasn't changed. He is there for you as He was for David. If God is willing to use you, you must let Him. You can't give up on yourself if He hasn't. You can't stop living, growing and contributing because you've sinned. There is nothing you can do about the past except forsake it and move on. It is over. You can't relive it and you can't obliterate it, but why should you let it affect the future? God doesn't want you to.

God wants to put your sins and iniquities as far from you as the east is from the west; to help you cope with the human condition. He wants you to do as David did: admit your sin, accept the responsibility for the results of it, then trust Him—the unchanging God—to help you rebound and live a meaningful, productive life.

REMEMBER: YOU ARE PHYSIOLOGICALLY AND EMOTIONALLY VULNERABLE BUT YOU AREN'T HOPELESS!

Workshop

Are you aware, as David was, of how deeply God cares about you? Are you condemning yourself? This workshop can help you sort out some areas where changes need to take place. Rate yourself with: A—always; O—often; S—sometimes; N—never.

1. I believe whatever God allows or causes to happen to me will be beneficial ___
2. I question why God has dealt with me in the way He has ___
3. I can't forgive myself so I can't expect God to forgive me ___
4. I think God is so angry and displeased with me that He is going to severely punish me ___
5. I believe God will forgive me no matter what I've done ___
6. I believe God is merciful and that He isn't trying to get back at me for my wrongdoings ___
7. I believe when bad things happen to me that God has made them happen ___
8. I believe God knows it will take time and effort for me to develop a steadfast spirit ___
9. I have failed so many times I'm certain God has given up on me ___
10. I believe God wants to love and help me more than retaliate against me ___
11. I think God understands my endurance, limitations and capabilities better than I do ___

Review carefully your answers to 2,3,4,7 and 9. Negative answers suggest you need to rethink the concepts in this chapter and make them a matter of special prayer. You may also want to discuss these problems with your pastor, or some other close Christian friend.

Note

1. H.D. Spence and T.S. Excell, *Psalms* Pulpit Commentary (Grand Rapids: Wm. B. Eerdmans Publishing Co., 1959), p. 63.

PARDON ME, 9
YOUR SELF-IMAGE
IS SHOWING

"I thought I had a good self-image, until you did the last session of your seminar," a lady said to me at a women's retreat. "When you compared Ruth's good self-image with Naomi's bad self-image, almost without exception, everything you said about Naomi is true about me. It's no wonder my husband is ready to leave me and my children avoid me when they can. I've been a miserable person to live with, but that's going to change." She had tears in her eyes as she asked me to pray for her.

She was referring to the concluding part of the study I'm going to share with you now. When I first decided to develop a study on the topic of self-image, I immediately turned to the book of Ruth, remembering that it embodied two women who had distinctly different attitudes about themselves and life in general. Naomi was a negative, defeated person and Ruth was optimistic and zealous. They can serve as an object lesson because they are classic examples of the difference between a bad and a good self-image.

This chapter will be a bit different from the others in that all of the written involvement comes at the end. As you read, see what you can learn about yourself as you examine the lives of these two women. Are you a Ruth or a Naomi?

A Crisis Situation

"Now it came about in the days when the judges governed, that there was a famine in the land." In the first words of chapter 1 of the book of Ruth we find there is a crisis situation—a famine. Little or no food was being produced and people were dying of starvation. The present was insecure and the future seemed hopeless.

Crisis situations are real tests for your self-image. Your actions and reactions when you are under stress indicate a good or bad self-image. Do you stay on top of the situation or go under? Act with relatively good sense or fall apart? Think for a minute how you behave in a crisis, major or minor.

A person with a good self-image usually retains his composure and performs in spite of the odds. That is what Elimelech, Naomi's husband, did in a crisis: "A certain man of Bethlehem in Judah went to sojourn in the land of Moab with his wife and two sons. And the name of the man was Elimelech, and the name of his wife was Naomi; and the names of his two sons were Mahlon and Chilion, Ephrathites of Bethlehem in Judah. Now they entered the land of Moab and re-

144

mained there" (Ruth 1:1,2). Elimelech moved his family so they could find food.

Naomi had her husband to lean on. She did not have to face her adequacy or inadequacy alone. It helps to have someone to depend on during times of crises. But there are some crises in your life you must face alone—no one else can help you bear them. When you are, by circumstance, forced to look yourself squarely in the eyes and say, "This is me," then you will discover the true fabric of your being. Naomi was soon thrown into just such a situation.

"Then Elimelech, Naomi's husband, died; and she was left with her two sons" (Ruth 1:3). So Naomi was living in a foreign land and was faced with the insecurity of widowhood. She did, however, have her sons, and they married, enlarging the family circle. "They took for themselves Moabite women as wives; the name of the one was Orpah and the name of the other Ruth. And they lived there about ten years. Then both Mahlon and Chilion also died; and the woman was bereft of her two children and her husband" (Ruth 1:4,5).

So Naomi's crisis deepened. She inherited the responsibility of heading her family. She was caught in one of those situations where she had to sink or swim. She wasn't left alone; as tragic as her loss was she still had her daughters-in-law. She was an Israelite so she also had the Lord.

What would you do in such a crisis? Would you turn toward God and cry, "Lord, I am going to rely on you to carry me through this," or would you hang your head and say, "I can't make it." Your perspective in a crisis reflects your self-image; do you look Godward or inward? What did Naomi do?

145

A Change of Scene

"Then she arose with her daughters-in-law that she might return from the land of Moab, for she had heard in the land of Moab that the Lord had visited His people in giving them food. So she departed from the place where she was, and her two daughters-in-law with her; and they went on the way to return to the land of Judah" (Ruth 1:6,7). On the surface it looks like Naomi was handling the situation very well. Since things had changed at home and the famine was over, she was going to go back to a more secure situation; she was going to change her scene.

In many cases it is a good idea to change the scene. Some people say, "Don't run from your problems." You *can't* run from your problems, but sometimes changing your setting alleviates the pain. Naomi couldn't reverse the fact that she was a widow or that she had lost her sons, but she could move into a setting that was more comfortable, where she felt more secure. Sometimes changing the scene will help you perform more capably.

Let's concentrate for a moment on Orpah and Ruth. Rather than retreating into a more secure situation, they were striking out into the unknown. They were leaving their home and roots and, out of loyalty to their husbands' mother, traveling to a foreign country. They were also widows and had suffered grief and loneliness. But "they went on the way to return to the land of Judah." They apparently had no qualms about going.

If you have a good self-image you won't fear the unknown but will live each day as it comes, trusting God for whatever happens. You rely on the omniscience of God. You may not know what the future holds but you know Who holds the future. One would think that

Naomi would have been delighted. She had made a decision; she was going home. Ruth and Orpah were accompanying her and she had every reason to believe the worst was over.

What was her attitude? "And Naomi said to her two daughters-in-law, 'Go, return each of you to her mother's house. May the Lord deal kindly with you as you have dealt with the dead and with me. May the Lord grant that you may find rest, each in the house of her husband.' Then she kissed them, and they lifted up their voices and wept" (Ruth 1:8,9).

On the surface it seems that Naomi was motivated by love in sending her daughters-in-law back to their own homes. But Naomi was being a bit of a martyr. In essence she was saying, "You girls stay here with your mothers and find a husband while I go on alone."

Naomi obviously realized that Orpah and Ruth were special people. She commended them for having been good wives and wished them happiness. On the other hand she was also selfishly insensitive to dismiss them the way she did.

Ruth and Orpah loved Naomi. They didn't want to leave her. There was no law or custom that said they had to go with Naomi, and Naomi was so important to them that they wanted to go with her. But Naomi didn't think she was valuable or important; she missed her own worth. Because she thought so poorly of herself she shut them out. She had a bad self-image that caused her to reject the love and affection of people who badly wanted to share her life. She blocked vital lines of communication and ended up a martyr. She couldn't understand how anybody could like her.

So what did Orpah and Ruth do when Naomi rejected

them. "They said to her, 'No, but we will surely return with you to your people' " (Ruth 1:10). There are several deep implications in that emphatic statement.

First, they both loved Naomi more than they did their own mothers.

Second, Naomi was dearer to them than the security of their homes.

The most obvious implication is that Naomi was so important to them that Ruth and Orpah truly wanted to go with her.

How would you respond if someone said that kind of no to you? I know what I'd do. I'd heave a sigh of relief and say, "Okay, let's go." But Naomi was a martyr. She enjoyed suffering. So she said, "Return, my daughters. Why should you go with me? Have I yet sons in my womb, that they may be your husbands? Return, my daughters! Go, for I am too old to have a husband. If I said I have hope, if I should even have a husband tonight and also bear sons, would you therefore wait until they were grown? Would you therefore refrain from marrying? No, my daughters; for it is harder for me than for you, for the hand of the Lord has gone forth against me" (Ruth 1:11-13).

Naomi the Negative

Now you gain a deeper insight into Naomi's sense of self. She made some very revealing statements in her dreary responses.

First, Naomi asked, "Why should you go with me?" In other words, she implied that she wasn't worth anything to Ruth and Orpah. It didn't dawn on her that they weren't interested in what she could do for them but that they loved her for herself. Isn't that a reflection of a poor self-image? Naomi thought that if they couldn't use her they wouldn't want her.

Then again, this may also be a backdoor way of asking for assurance. Insecure people negatively search for compliments. The wife who says, "I really fixed a lousy dinner tonight, didn't I?" or the student who tells her teacher, "You won't like my report," are both seeking approval.

Next, Naomi bewailed the fact that she couldn't provide husbands for them if they should want to remarry. She then concludes by saying, "It is harder for me than it is for you, for the hand of the Lord has gone out against me" (Ruth 1:13). By whose standards was it harder for her than for Orpah or Ruth?

She made this presumptuous observation because she was bogged down in self-pity, a product of a poor self-image. She operated on the premise that she was not worth much, therefore no one wanted or needed her.

Then Naomi concluded with, "Why did this happen to me?" The final step in the cycle of self-pity is to blame somebody else for your inadequacies. Naomi blamed God. Instead of facing reality, she believed that the hand of the Lord had gone out against her. It's all God's fault. There is no doubt that God had His hand on Naomi's life, but she didn't look at the situation from His divine perspective and try to see what His intentions were. Instead, she cursed her fate and inconsiderately hurt Ruth and Orpah, so much so that "they lifted up their voices and wept again" (Ruth 1:14).

Ruth the Optimist

Naomi's demands finally forced a decision. "Orpah kissed her mother-in-law, but Ruth clung to her" (Ruth

149

1:14). Orpah left. I think I'd have been inclined to do the same. But Ruth stayed. Undaunted, she ignored Naomi's protests and refused to go. By her actions Ruth showed that she had a good self-image. She was able to stick to what she believed. A person with a good self-image doesn't have to be dogmatic or opinionated but is confident and secure about what she is doing and why she is doing it.

How did Naomi respond to Ruth's love and loyalty? "She said, 'Behold, your sister-in-law has gone back to her people and her gods; return after your sister-in-law' " (Ruth 1:15). Naomi hadn't given up yet! She rejected Ruth again.

Her action portrays the principle we discussed in a previous chapter: You can't accept others if you can't accept yourself. Self-rejection makes you reject other people, even those whom you need and love. Naomi didn't want to be alone. She wanted Ruth to go with her but she pushed her away because of her own insecurity.

Someone with less character and understanding than Ruth would have given up. "But Ruth said, 'Do not urge me to leave you or turn back from following you; for where you go, I will go, and where you lodge, I will lodge. Your people shall be my people, and your God, my God. Where you die, I will die, and there I will be buried. Thus may the Lord do to me, and worse, if anything but death parts you and me' " (Ruth 1:16,17).

Ruth's words have been quoted through the ages as the supreme example of loyalty, conviction and determination. Because she had a good self-image, she had the strength and courage to take such a stand. A person with a good self-image can act on principles apart from the personalities and the people who are involved.

So Ruth went with her mother-in-law, despite the persistent demand of Naomi that she stay. Ruth realized that she had an obligation—not to her mother-in-law but to the Lord. A person with a good self-image can set her mind to do God's will and not capitulate to what people want. If Ruth had not gone with Naomi, she would not have been included in the messianic line. Ruth didn't know that. But because she was true to herself and her convictions, God blessed her.

There must have been many things Ruth knew about Naomi. She had been with her for over 10 years. She must have sensed that Naomi was afraid, insecure and lonely. She probably knew how desperately Naomi needed a companion.

Because Ruth had a good self-image she didn't feel she had to struggle to survive or to exert herself; therefore she could be sensitive and could properly minister to Naomi. A person who isn't always worried about how she is going to subsist can be concerned with what is happening to others. She can see the grief in people's eyes when there are smiles on their faces. Ruth was that kind of person.

Ruth was also a leader. Her good self-image helped her take the initiative. A good leader doesn't always have to be the one who is running the show, but the true mark of leadership is being able to take charge when necessary and to give direction by delegating authority. Ruth wasn't worried about what Naomi thought. She saw what needed to be done and she did it. She could effectively serve others because she had confidence in herself.

Naomi wasn't much help to herself or anyone else. She caused problems for Orpah and Ruth. Ruth, on the other hand, knew she had something to offer, that she could help Naomi.

If you are afraid to give of yourself, to let go of bits and pieces of yourself and to plug into other people's lives, you'll never be able to adequately serve them.

A person with good self-image is free to serve others.

Naomi the Bitter

So the women left for Bethlehem. "When [Naomi] saw that [Ruth] was determined to go with her, she said no more to her. So they both went until they came to Bethlehem. And it came about when they had come to Bethlehem, that all the city was stirred because of them, and the women said, 'Is this Naomi?' " (Ruth 1:18,19). Can't you see that happening? You know how small towns are—everyone concerned about everyone else's affairs. So when Ruth and Naomi and her household came into town, the people were curious. The women, probably former friends, couldn't believe Naomi was really back.

You'd think Naomi would have been overjoyed to have completed the trip and be home again. Instead she greeted her friends and neighbors with a morose rebuttal: "Do not call me Naomi; call me Mara, for the Almighty has dealt very bitterly with me. I went out full, but the Lord has brought me back empty. Why do you call me Naomi, since the Lord has witnessed against me and the Almighty has afflicted me?" (Ruth 1:20,21).

What Naomi said reveals a great deal about her self-image. First she said, "Don't call me Naomi." Do you know why? Because Naomi means "pleasant," and she was certainly being anything but that.

Then she told them to call her Mara, which means

"bitter." Our English derivative of *mara* is the word martyr. Naomi is a classic example of a martyr. She typifies what loss of self-esteem can do to a person. She had no joy, saw no positives and had changed from a pleasant woman into a bitter martyr. The end result was that she blamed God. *He* caused the bitterness. *He* afflicted her. *He* made her empty.

A person with a poor self-image can't cope with problems in a positive way. She is defeated before she tries.

Ruth the Doer

So Ruth and Naomi were at home in Bethlehem and it was the beginning of the barley harvest. I'm sure Ruth was uneasy. She didn't know what would happen when she went to Bethlehem. She had a martyr for a mother-in-law. She was a widow in a strange land but, unlike Naomi, she didn't sit around bemoaning her fate. She made the most of her circumstances.

"Now Naomi had a kinsman of her husband, a man of great wealth . . . whose name was Boaz. And Ruth the Moabitess said to Naomi, 'Please let me go to the field and glean among the ears of grain after one in whose sight I may find favor.' And she said to her, 'Go, my daughter.' So she departed and went and gleaned in the field after the reapers; and she happened to come to the portion of the field belonging to Boaz, who was of the family of Elimelech" (Ruth 2:1-3).

Ruth was a doer. She wanted to use her capabilities and talents.

A person with a good self-image probably is a busy person, actively involved in doing profitable things. If a person has a poor self-image she may superficially perform, but will be bored and dissatisfied and frequently inactive because she doesn't want to risk failure.

Ruth went to work in the fields and Boaz, who happened to be there that day, saw her and wanted to know who she was. "Then Boaz said to his servant who was in charge of the reapers, 'Whose young woman is this?' " (Ruth 2:5). His foreman told him she was Naomi's daughter-in-law from Moab.

Boaz had heard about her so he went to her and lovingly issued a warning. "Then Boaz said to Ruth, 'Listen, carefully, my daughter. Do not go to glean in another field; furthermore, do not go on from this one, but stay here with my maids. Let your eyes be on the field which they reap, and go after them. Indeed, *I have commanded the servants not to touch you.* When you are thirsty, go to the water jars and drink from what the servants draw' "(Ruth 2:8,9, italics added).

Sounds rather ominous, doesn't it? Obviously, the field workers didn't like foreigners or intruders. Boaz was afraid they might threaten or hurt her so he gave specific instructions to insure her safety.

How did Ruth handle this potentially dangerous situation? She didn't worry and she didn't withdraw. She didn't say, "What do you mean you told them not to touch me? What's the matter? What could happen to me?" Instead, "She fell on her face, bowing to the ground and said to him, 'Why have I found favor in your sight that you should take notice of me, since I am a foreigner?' " (Ruth 2:10).

She focused on Boaz's positive action rather than the negative circumstances. She graciously accepted what Boaz had done for her. "And Boaz answered and said to her, 'All that you have done for your mother-in-law after the death of your husband has been fully reported

154

to me, and how you left your father and your mother and the land of your birth, and came to a people you did not previously know. May the Lord reward your work, and your wages be full from the Lord, the God of Israel, under whose wings you have come to seek refuge' " (Ruth 2:11,12). What a statement!

A person with a good self-image shows it in her performance, just as Ruth did. She who seeks refuge under the wings of the Lord doesn't have to worry about what might happen or what other people might say or do. She doesn't have to seek rewards or notoriety. God will publicize what she does. He is all-sufficient and emotional and physical "wages" come from Him.

Too often a person with a poor self-image does good things not to serve but to be noticed. She expects recognition in return. When there is no response her ego is deflated. She thinks, "Just look what I did for them and they don't appreciate it. They don't like me. But why should they—look who I am."

What was Ruth's reply to Boaz's compliment? "I have found favor in your sight, my lord, for you have comforted me and indeed have spoken kindly to your maidservant, though I am not like one of your maidservants" (Ruth 2:13). This is the first actual indication that things hadn't been easy for Ruth. She needed to be comforted and consoled. She had encountered her share of problems, but she hadn't let them destroy her confidence nor affect her performance. Having a good self-image didn't eliminate her hurts and frustrations, but she was able to cope in a constructive way.

Ruth also knew how to accept a compliment. She appreciated what Boaz said and responded graciously to his glowing remarks. A person with a strong self-image can handle compliments. She can accept valid, positive compliments and respond with an appropriate, honest statement. A person with a weak self-image will be embarrassed, become flustered or deny that what was said is true, because she finds it difficult to face positives about herself. She may feel compelled to return a compliment, whether it is warranted or not.

Ruth's story has a happy ending. She worked in the fields until the barley and wheat harvests were over and, eventually, "Boaz took Ruth, and she became his wife, and he went in to her. And the Lord enabled her to conceive, and she gave birth to a son" (Ruth 4:13). Her son was Obed, who had a son named Jesse, who had a son named David, who became king of Israel. She was one of the three women Matthew named in his account of the messianic lineage (see Matt. 1:5-7). If she had been like Naomi she would never have left Moab and another woman would have received God's blessing.

It's important to note that God didn't supernaturally force Ruth to go with Naomi. He didn't send an angel to instruct her with, "Ruth, the Lord commands you to go with Naomi." She developed her potential and God used her because she was pliable, self-assured and capable.

In closing, let's summarize the characteristics of self-image that were evident in these two women.

Naomi showed her poor self-image by her	*Ruth showed her good self-image by her*
martyrdom	giving attitude
lack of self-worth	realization of self-worth
rejection of others	acceptance of others
self-pity	ability to take a stand about
depression	what she believed

insensitivity to others	strength and courage to
making God (or circum-	follow her principles
stances) the scapegoat	ability to cope with
inability to cope with	positives
stresses or problems	priorities
selfishness	leadership qualities
impotent relationships	help to others
worry	ability to cope with stresses
	and problems
	godliness
	fruitful relationships
	peace of mind

What encouragement can you draw from this study of Ruth and Naomi? Probably the greatest one is that you have a choice. Naomi could have chosen to remain "pleasant" rather than becoming bitter. Ruth could have turned her back on Naomi and done the easy thing, but she didn't.

If you gain nothing else from this book but the encouragement that you can become the person you would like to be, then you have taken a step forward on the long, and sometimes tedious, road to self-acceptance. Obviously, there is no panacea or pat formula that will instantly and irrevocably restructure your self-image. But if you are willing to divert your attentions from your shortcomings and weaknesses and onto God and invest some time and effort, you can overcome many of your problems.

You have a choice. With God's help you can improve your self-concept and learn to value yourself. You can forgive yourself and eradicate guilt. It *is* possible.

The apostle Paul, in 2 Peter 1:2,3, penned this beautiful, Spirit-inspired thought: "Grace and peace be multiplied to you in the knowledge of God and of Jesus our Lord; seeing that His divine power has granted to us everything pertaining to life and godliness, through the true knowledge of Him who called us by His own glory and excellence."

Through God's power and a knowledge of Christ, you have *everything* you need to live a rich, full, happy, confident, godly life. Believe it! Act on it! The choice is yours.

REMEMBER: YOU CAN CHOOSE TO BE A RUTH OR A NAOMI. WHICH WILL IT BE?

Workshop

Are you a Ruth or a Naomi? This workshop will let you compare your self-image quotient to theirs. Rate yourself below with the following scale: N—never; S—sometimes; U—usually; A—always.

1. I handle crisis situations with relative ease ＿＿
2. I rely on myself more than on other people ＿＿
3. I am self-sufficient ＿＿
4. I look to God as the primary and most reliant resource for help ＿＿
5. I am secure and don't worry about the past or the future ＿＿
6. I am affectionate and am not afraid to show my feelings ＿＿
7. I can graciously accept a compliment ＿＿
8. I refuse to feel sorry for myself ＿＿
9. I believe that I, not God, am responsible for my inadequacies ＿＿
10. I do what I think is right rather than what is expected of me ＿＿

158

11. I stick to what I believe ___
12. I am sensitive to the unspoken, subtle needs of others. ___
13. I like to do things for others ___
14. I am actively involved in doing what I consider to be worthwhile activities ___
15. I can find positives in negative situations ___
16. I can do almost anything if I put my mind to it ___
17. I cope with frustrations in a positive way ___
18. I realize my self-worth ___
19. I have peace of mind ___
20. I accept others at face value ___

To tally your score, give yourself 0 for each *never*, 1 point for each *sometimes*, 2 points for *usually* and 3 points for each *always*.

If you have a score of 50-60 you may be fooling yourself, or bordering on a giant attack of ego. If your score is in the 35-50 range, you have a balanced, realistic sense of self-esteem. A score of 25-35 means you have about an equal amount of self-worth and insecurity but there is still room for improvement. You need to concentrate on enhancing your self-image in the areas where you scored lowest. If you scored in the 15-25 range, your self-image definitely needs a boost. You need to isolate and reverse the negative patterns that are pulling you down. If you fall in the 0-15 range, you need to consistently use the self-helps suggested in this book and perhaps seek counsel from your pastor or someone you trust to help you eliminate your problems.